FRANK W. WILSON

FRANK W. WILSON

NEIL THOMAS

Library of Congress Control Number:		2020908835
ISBN:	Hardcover	978-1-9845-7932-4
	Softcover	978-1-9845-7931-7
	eBook	978-1-9845-7930-0

Print information available on the last page.

Rev. date: 07/07/2020

To order additional copies of this book, contact:
Xlibris
1-888-795-4274
www.Xlibris.com
Orders@Xlibris.com
807779

CONTENTS

FOREWORD

Every year in January, I come into my chambers alone, uninterrupted, for at least two hours, and I ask myself the question, "Over the last year, have I abused my Article III powers in any way?"

—Frank Wiley Wilson,
United States District Judge

It is easy for a judge to become unrestrained in the exercise of judicial power, especially a federal judge, whose term of office is limited only by impeachment. For a judge who has become infatuated by the position, this question is never asked. It is a judge whose hallmark is humility who asks the question whether he has abused the power conferred upon him by Article III of the Constitution of the United States. Judge Frank Wilson asked himself this question every year, fearing that he might have, in some way, abused that power.

Frank Wiley Wilson was an unforgettable man of extraordinary qualities, which will be seen in his decisions, his courtroom demeanor, his speeches, and his high regard for his fellow human being. Aside from his many qualities of impartiality, devotion to justice, humility, patience, wisdom, and humor, he had the common touch. He never lost sight of what was expected from individuals in their social interactions, not merely in terms of which conduct was then condemned but also which conduct was then expected in the relationship among fellow human beings.

His determination to do what was right was what led Judge Wilson to ask himself this question each new year—whether the power possessed had been abused. For a judge to use that introspection is a reflection of his understanding of the power of the position that is held.

So as we travel through his life, we will see everything Frank Wilson did or urged others to do and how it would be governed by the exercise of fairness.

There is one sentence in one of his decisions that exhibits his wisdom better than perhaps any other. That decision was in the case of *Mapp v. Board of Education of the City of Chattanooga*. The case involved the desegregation of Chattanooga City schools in the 1960s, and it occurred during the public outcry aftermath in the South over the Supreme Court's unanimous 1954 decision in *Brown v. Board of Education*. Until *Brown*, the Supreme Court had permitted the doctrine of "separate but equal" to decide whether equal protection existed between the races in the field of education. Before *Brown*, the Supreme Court had held that, as long as the treatment of blacks was equal to that of whites, the races could be separate without considering whether separate equality was, in reality, inequality. In *Brown*, the Supreme Court brought that rule to an end. And in Chattanooga, *Mapp* brought that rule to a finale.

To those, however, who criticized the Supreme Court's unanimous decision, Judge Wilson said, "How many are so convinced of the correctness of their own interpretation of that clause that they would be willing to live in a society where each man is free to make his own interpretation of laws. Surely thoughtful men must agree that the rule of law is the single greatest achievement of the country's long struggle for freedom."

But then as he often did, Judge Wilson framed the constitutional issue—the application of the equal protection clause of the Fourteenth Amendment of the Constitution—in practical terms. In asking the question, Are all children in the Chattanooga City schools receiving an equal education? he posed a simple answer to a difficult question when he said,

> Quality education might not seem so difficult for anyone to maintain if it were truly his brother's child that was being deprived or handicapped by its denial.

This inspired the title of this book.

ACKNOWLEDGMENTS

The author wishes to acknowledge the Baker Center at the University of Tennessee for access to the archives, which included Judge Wilson's papers, and to the law firms of Miller & Martin, and Chambliss & Bahner for their financial contribution. Finally, the author is most grateful to the following, who patiently read and offered advice with respect to this biography: Randy and Pamela Wilson, Debra Arfkin, and Jane Bowen.

CHAPTER ONE

Young Frank

Frank Wiley Wilson was born in the latter days of World War I on June 21, 1917, to Frank Caldwell and Mary Wiley Wilson in Knoxville, Tennessee. His family was originally from North Carolina. The North Carolina Wiley family, from which he drew his genes, had an illustrious background. During the Civil War, his great-grandfather, W. M. Wiley, had written to then Col. Zebulon Vance, offering to form a North Carolina cavalry unit for the Confederacy. Colonel Vance, who later would become governor of North Carolina both before and after the Civil War, responded to Mr. Wiley's offer.

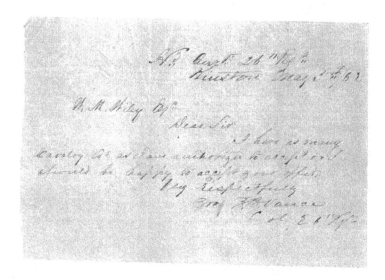

For the summers while in high school, young Frank continued his North Carolina heritage by working in his Uncle Wiley's farm near Greensboro, North Carolina, where he would rise at four thirty in the morning to milk twelve cows. Back in high school in Knoxville, he walked a four-mile newspaper route and graduated in 1934.

In addition, he played the trombone in the marching band, a pastime that stayed with him and relaxed him for the rest of his life. His family recalled that during stressful times after he became a judge, he would often relax by retreating to the basement to play his trombone.

Following graduation, Frank started on a road to numerous achievements—graduating from the University of Tennessee in 1939 summa cum laude with dual bachelor of arts degrees in history and political science. He was inducted into Phi Beta Kappa and the military honor society of Scabbard and Blade and was a member of the University of Tennessee debate team.

SUCCESSFU L DEBATERS

Photo by Christenberry.

The U-T Debating Club which, divided into two groups, made tours of the middle and eastern sections of the state last week, winning all of their meets, and bringing glory to the institution. From left to right, they are: Leonard Rogers, Nancy Poore, Fran Bass, Thomas McKinney, Henry Carmichael, Gene Liggett, James Allison, Dr. John B. Emperor, coach, and Frank Wilson.

Frank followed his undergraduate degree with a law degree from the University of Tennessee Law School in 1941. Not satisfied with having graduated from the University of Tennessee with honors (cum laude), he graduated from the law school summa cum laude. He was also awarded a faculty scholarship and added to his accolades by being the editor of the law review, which he achieved by being first in his law school class.

Frank was admitted to the bar in 1941 and practiced for a short while in Knoxville with the law firm of Poore, Kramer & Cox until reporting for military service on March 21, 1941. There, he hoped to be assigned to the Judge Advocate branch. Because the report date on his notice had been transposed by a clerk, however, he was late in reporting for duty and was assigned to the Army Air Corps and sent to North Africa and Italy. Before shipping out, he married his bride of forty years, Helen Warwick, of Knoxville on April 6, 1942.

CHAPTER TWO

The War Years

We made it totally impossible for democracy to work in Germany after the last war and reaped a demagogue of the worst sort as a result.

—Frank Wilson, letter to his mother

Although Frank Wilson's education laurels clearly showed his intellectual side, there was also a side to him that was sensitive to human plight. The real tragedy of World War II, as he saw it, was the impact upon the lives of people. He saw people who were living through the war, not just fighting it, and the land that suffered the scars from the machinery of war. He often saw the war in the pitiful children in rags in war-torn Italy and the once beautiful but now devastated countryside.

His military experience began with basic training at Fort Riley, Kansas, where he attained the rank of corporal, a rank from which he was promoted to sergeant by the end of the war.

Officers, he wrote, were accorded privileged treatment, while enlisted men simply occupied space:

When he was shipped overseas, his trip abroad was on an unescorted troop ship, and his crossing was miserable. In a letter home to Helen, he focused on the difference in the treatment of enlisted men and officers.

> To begin with, we came over on a navy troopship and came alone...We were crowded into a hole with about 600 men to a compartment. A compartment is about 50 × 60 feet. Bunks are in tiers, five to a tier...As I mentioned, discipline was much stricter on some ships, and the difference between officers and enlisted men was never greater. 600 officers were given more space than 6,000 men, and all the decks were turned over to the officers exclusively. We were kept in the hole for two weeks straight until sickness for some caused them to open part of the deck to enlisted men. Then we got to go on the forward deck for two hours a day.

Shortly after his arrival in Europe, he wrote home about "D-Day" on the actual date of D-Day, June 6, 1944, merely noting that "this was quite a day—the invasion began."

After landing in Africa, his unit was shipped to Italy, and Frank worked his way up the Italian Peninsula where he ended at Paloma, where he was instrumental in the start-up of Paloma Tech, which was the subject of a story by a war correspondent, Robert St. John of the

National Broadcasting Company (NBC). On April 5, 1945, St. John wrote about the unique Army project in which Frank Wilson was a key figure. St. John had been told about Paloma by NBC's Italian correspondent Grant Parr, who said the school, which was the largest army school anywhere in Italy, was a preview of the way army colleges would be run in Europe for victorious American soldiers after V-E Day. The colleges had been planned for the soldiers to fill a void because of a prediction that it would take four to six months after Germany's collapse to ship the soldiers back to the United States or to the Pacific. That wait, doing nothing, would have been devastating for morale. So it would be back to school for both officers and soldiers. But air headquarters got the jump on that program, and twenty-eight soldiers and officers were selected to be teachers at Paloma Tech, and they taught an enrollment of six hundred, two nights a week. The school grew to even have its own basketball team. Its president was a captain from Andover, Massachusetts, but according to St. John, "the hardest-working man on the faculty is Cpl. Frank Wilson of Knoxville, Tennessee, because besides teaching two classes, he is the administrative assistant of the school. Corporal Wilson used to practice law in Knoxville."

The protocol at the school was a bit different from the rest of the armed services because students and teachers checked their rank at the door. One rather humorous rule of the school was that colonels under the age of twenty-one who were late for class had to have a written excuse from a general. Frank Wilson himself described the school in a May 9, 1945, letter to Helen: "As I've tried to explain before, my work is in the Information and Education Section and my job here is to handle all the education and orientation work in the squadron...Together we operate all extra duty activities on the post—the movies, the snack bar, the dayroom, the bar, all athletics, the library, the orientation work in the school. At present we aren't operating the school as we finished one semester and are waiting for things to settle down before opening again."

After having been the subject of the story by NBC in April of 1945, Frank wrote home in May 1945, not about the education of American soldiers but rather about the children he saw. He poignantly described them—the people and their children and the horrors he saw in a war-torn Italy:

> Pathetic kids stare up at you with faces covered with sores, half-blind eyes, and their scrawny bodies covered only with rags, usually just from the waist up. All are begging for caramelly (candy) or just anything you will give them. Even a match, a single match, is a luxury. You look at these people and ask, Are these the enemy? Are these the ones we wanted to punish for fascism and the war? Is this what we came over here to fight? Is this the sort of revenge that is going to make the world a better place to live in?

In that letter, he questioned why the motives of the leaders of nations appeared to be opposite to the needs of their people. Why, he wondered, did this all have to happen? Frank Wilson would constantly raise the question "why" when things did not seem to make sense.

> It is rather difficult to understand why problems which seem so fundamentally easy to solve are causing such hair-tearing concern to the world leaders. You can only suspect that their frantic efforts are just to cover their own conscience. For example, take the efforts to effect a stable peace. They talk of peace, but there is no peace—and it just isn't peace they really want. Instead, they want only armed suppression, with the "right people" on the top.

With almost exquisite foreign policy insight, he again questioned why we do things and persist in doing things wrongly:

> The blunders committed after the last war which made this one almost inevitable are all being repeated this time, only on a much grander scale and without any vestige of a Wilson crying in the wilderness and appealing to the world's conscience. We made it totally impossible for democracy to work in Germany after the last war and reaped a demagogue of the worst sort as a result.

After all, the "definition of insanity is doing the same thing over and over again but expecting a different result" (Albert Einstein).

When the war finally came to an end in Europe, Frank Wilson did not see the exhilaration depicted back home on the movie screen. There was no media hype, no kissing in Times Square. He wrote to Helen:

> Yesterday we got the official announcement of V-E Day through President Truman's address. I thought he made a rather poor address considering the occasion. There is little sign of exhilaration or celebration over here. Everyone is beginning to "sweat out" the Pacific, though we are each hoping to be lucky enough to go through the States.

By the end of the war, he had migrated from Paloma to Caserta, Italy. His headquarters was located in King's Palace, a seventeenth-century structure that had, at one time, sported magnificent grounds with waterfalls, statuary, manicured lawns, and monuments. The palace itself had four large inner courtyards and an opera house. It headquartered all ground, naval, and air force operations for the entire Mediterranean. Thus, he wrote, "Generals are as thick here as Lieutenants."

Although in the theaters at home the newsreels may have glamorized the end of the war, for Frank Wilson and his location, it was a low-key and nonspectacular end of the war in Europe. The servicemen at King's Palace did not even know of the German surrender until a week after it had happened, and for their section of the war theater, it had actually happened at King's Palace. He wrote to Helen, "The surrender here in Italy was signed at the palace Sunday week ago, but we knew nothing about it until it was announced to the world Wednesday. The German officers came in civilian clothes."

Corporal Wilson did have an opportunity to do some traveling during his tour in Italy, but what he saw, he did not like. Two letters, in particular, one to Helen and one to his mother, described the ravages of Rome and Naples. The juxtaposition of the reconstruction of churches, in particular, was despairingly compared with the horrible loss of life.

In describing the abbey and the Battle of Monte Cassino, he lamented over the monumental loss of life and the enormous expenditure made to restore the church when the Italian people lacked so much:

> The remains of the abbey stand out on the mountain just behind the town. Five companies were wiped out trying to climb the mountain before the abbey was bombed—and afterwards it was just the same. All along the road and through the town are graves and graveyards and German, British, and American alike. One grave strikes you harder than 100 destroyed abbeys—yet the abbey made headlines all over the world. Now the church is going to spend $5 million to rebuild it. Maybe they can finish it in time to say mass in it for 5 million Italians that will starve if the United States doesn't feed them.

Finally, he questioned and condemned the misallocation of resources:

> Never was a country so rich in churches and so poor in people as this. Bare feet on marble floors and tattered clothes among majestic columns look incongruous to say the least, and drawn wrinkled and furled faces and hard, sad eyes look all the more tragic in the light of stained-glass windows.

Then he wrote of his visit to Naples:

> Though I have grown quite accustomed to sites that at one time shocked me speechless, I've never been able to become accustomed to the sites that I see in Naples—and in many ways the conditions of Naples are typical of all Southern Italy. The extremes are just more exaggerated there.

He started with the beauty he saw:

> Nature created Naples one of the most beautiful spots on earth. The great circular harbor is surrounded by wonderful hills, and it is truly an awe-inspiring site to stand up on the hills in the Palermo section, that is, the Northern part of the

city, and look out over the city below, with the sky-blue water stretching out across the horizon, interrupted only by the jutting up of the hazy blue island of Capri and with Vesuvius reaching to the clouds just back of the city.

But then for Frank Wilson, the war intruded on Naples:

> You mustn't look too close, though, for you begin to see what man has done to all of this—and it isn't pretty, not at all. You can't help but see the ugliness, for it surrounds you. In fact, you must shut it out of your mind to see any of the beauty.

Although concerned about the bombing and the destruction of the Italian countryside, Frank was more concerned about the people. He wrote to Helen:

> I don't know just how the Italian people feel toward us. They don't love us. Certainly, some of them hate us. Most of them just accept us. They seem to feel about the same way against the Germans, though of course they talk a strong line against them when they want something. Further north I think it is different. Most Italians hate Mussolini—probably just because he led them into a losing war.

This graphic description was continued in the November 1945 letter to his mother:

> I saw that again firsthand yesterday, and no matter how many times you have seen it before, you don't get used to it—it is as though you have seen it for the first time, and each time, it seems to hurt a little worse, way down inside. You can't believe they are humans nor even animals, for animals can't live so miserably. It is rather like something Dante imagined for his *Inferno*.
>
> The diseases that wracked these people must be unknown to the medical books. I saw one old man who was undoubtedly the most ghastly sight I've ever seen. His flesh was all

completely gone, and great shreds of raw or dead flesh hung down from his face and jaws—and yet he lived. Many others may have been dead; they lay so motionless. Pathetic kids stare up at you with faces covered with sores, half-blind eyes, and their scrawny bodies covered with rags, usually just from the waist up.

And then he ended with what would always be a concern to him as a human being and as a judge—the loss of hope:

> Miserable as their lives must be, surely the worst part of it all must be the utter hopelessness of their condition. Almost anything can be put up with for a while as long as there is a promise of things getting better...For most of these people, there is absolutely no promise of things ever being any better.

His letters have been quoted at some length with trepidation because, to some extent, their quotation involves an invasion of his privacy—communications to his wife and mother expressed innermost feelings. But they have been quoted because their beauty of expression, reflective of such profound but simple beliefs, overcomes any such trepidation. His experiences during the war in Italy undoubtedly had a profound effect upon Frank, who would constantly ask "why" all through his life when faced with a belief that may have been widely accepted but never questioned.

CHAPTER THREE

The Start of a Career and the Elevation to Judge

I hope that the lawyers and others who come in contact with this court will find it an agreeable place to work and practice your profession.

—Frank Wilson, Induction Ceremony

After his 1946 honorable discharge from the army, Frank Wilson started a law firm in Oak Ridge with his lifelong friend, Eugene Joyce. He practiced there from 1946 to 1961 and was president or chairman of every organization in town. He was also the first Oak Ridge resident elected to public office in Anderson County—that of county attorney. He founded the Bank of Oak Ridge, on whose board he served until he was appointed to the federal bench in 1961 by President John F. Kennedy.

Before his appointment to the federal bench, however, Frank Wilson was a highly successful trial attorney, having applied his skills well enough to obtain the largest jury verdict in the state of Tennessee at the time. His humor was evident long before his appointment to the bench as he recounted one of his cases, in which he represented a Knoxville bakery. The driver of the bakery truck was a man named Perry, who was accompanied by a ten-year-old boy he had picked up. Judge Wilson had some trouble qualifying the lad as competent to testify because of his innocence and tender years, but when the lad got on the witness stand and was asked what happened after he saw the approaching car, the boy of tender years replied, "Goddamn, Perry, we are going to hit him."

There are only four published appellate decisions of cases in which Frank Wilson was counsel and argued in the appellate courts; three were in the Supreme Court, and one was in the Court of Appeals. One case before the Supreme Court involved only the date from which interest would be calculated, but that case recited in its procedural history that Frank Wilson had recovered a judgment for his client in 1954 in the amount of $109,000; in today's dollars, that would be $1,000,000. In another case before the Supreme Court, Frank Wilson defended an ordinance of the city of Norris that prohibited a fence in front of a house higher than three feet. Although he was unsuccessful in convincing the Supreme Court of the constitutionality of the ordinance, the Court used a statement that Frank Wilson later humorously used about the inability to find a citation for a proposition of law. The phrase used by the Supreme Court when faced with being unable to find authority for a proposition was "It is too well settled to require further citation of authorities, that…" Perhaps Frank just borrowed this phrase later.

The remaining cases involved esoteric issues such as when the statute of limitations began to run in a worker's compensation case and whether a partnership may be established by the statement of one of the partners.

During those years of his practice, he hired a young associate, Riley Anderson, who later became a justice and then chief justice of the Supreme Court of the State of Tennessee. Justice Anderson remembers Frank Wilson as one of the hardest-working lawyers he had ever known and recounted that, although Frank Wilson was deeply religious, had it not been for his wife, Helen, and her requirement that the family attend church service every Sunday, Frank Wilson would have spent seven days in the office. This was the work ethic with which the lawyers who appeared before him would come to know—such as attending pretrial conferences on Christmas Eve day.

Many remember Frank Wilson as an avid student of the law and a community volunteer, but not many realize he was also deeply involved in politics, he himself running for Congress in 1950. He was a close friend of then congressman, then senator Al Gore Sr. and Senator Estes Kefauver.

HEADQUARTERS
—
COLONIAL HOTEL ARCADE
KNOXVILLE, TENN.
PHONE 3-9672

T o :

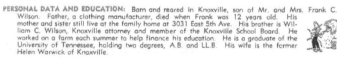

FRANK W. WILSON
for
UNITED STATES CONGRESS
(2ND CONGRESSIONAL DISTRICT)

Know Your Man ———————→

PERSONAL DATA AND EDUCATION: Born and reared in Knoxville, son of Mr. and Mrs. Frank C. Wilson. Father, a clothing manufacturer, died when Frank was 12 years old. His mother and sister still live at the family home at 3031 East 5th Ave. His brother is William C. Wilson, Knoxville attorney and member of the Knoxville School Board. He worked on a farm each summer to help finance his education. He is a graduate of the University of Tennessee, holding two degrees, A.B. and LL.B. His wife is the former Helen Warwick of Knoxville.

ARMY SERVICE: A World War II veteran of the Italian Campaign, with four years service in the U. S. Army, and he was honorably discharged in 1946.

PROFESSIONAL EXPERIENCE: He practiced law in Knoxville with a well-known law firm prior to entering military service in 1942, and returned to the same firm in 1946. That same year, he moved his law practice to Oak Ridge. He is currently a member of a Knoxville and Oak Ridge law firm. He has served as County Attorney for Anderson County since 1948.

CHURCH AFFILIATION: A member of the Fifth Ave. Presbyterian Church, Knoxville, and is affiliated with the United Church of Oak Ridge, where he has served as Chairman of the Board of Trustees, and teaches a Sunday School class.

CIVIC: He has served actively in the following offices: Commander of the American Legion; President, Better Business Association; Editor, Tennessee Law Review; President, Community Chest; Vice-President, Jr. Chamber of Commerce; Director, Chamber of Commerce; Chairman, Red Cross; Judge Advocate, Veterans of Foreign Wars; Director, Family Welfare Board; Treasurer, Bar Association; Chairman, Oak Ridge Incorporation Commission; Member, Oak Ridge Planning & Zoning Commission. He is also a member of the American Bar Association and the Tennessee Bar Association, Phi Delta Phi, Amvets, B.P.O.E., and Rotary Club.

HONORS: Graduated with highest honors in his law class, elected member of Phi Kappa Phi

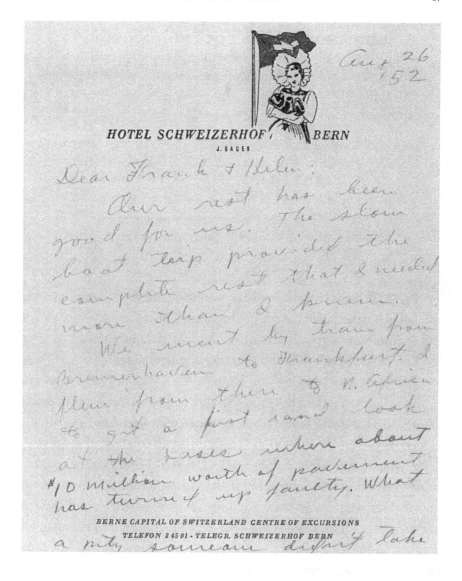

Frank Wilson was the Democratic nominee for Congress for the Second Congressional District. Although he lost to Howard Baker Sr., he came closer than any Democrat had ever done in a heavily Republican district, losing by roughly 3,000 votes out of 60,000.

Tennessee's 1950 Football Schedule

Sept. 23—Mississippi Southern ⎯⎯⎯⎯⎯ Here
Sept. 30—Mississippi State ⎯⎯⎯⎯⎯ Starkville
Oct.　7—Duke ⎯⎯⎯⎯⎯⎯⎯⎯⎯ Durham
Oct. 14—Chattanooga ⎯⎯⎯⎯⎯⎯ Here
Oct. 21—Alabama ⎯⎯⎯⎯⎯⎯⎯ Here
Oct. 28—Washington and Lee ⎯⎯⎯ Here
Nov.　4—North Carolina ⎯⎯⎯⎯⎯ Here
Nov.　7—ELECT FRANK WILSON TO CONGRESS
Nov. 11—Tennessee Tech ⎯⎯⎯⎯ Here
Nov. 18—Mississippi ⎯⎯⎯⎯⎯⎯ Here
Nov. 25—Kentucky ⎯⎯⎯⎯⎯⎯ Here
Dec.　2—Vanderbilt ⎯⎯⎯⎯⎯ Nashville

Frank Wilson also directed the statewide effort of Estes Kefauver when Senator Kefauver ran for President of the United States, for which the senator was deeply appreciative. Senator Kefauver would later be responsible for Frank Wilson becoming a federal judge.

For fourteen years, Frank built a private practice in Oak Ridge, ran a personal congressional campaign, and helped direct a presidential campaign. But then Frank Wilson considered an alternative path to his career. By December 5, 1960, his interest turned to a federal judgeship, as he wrote to then senators Gore and Kefauver, "I find that the rewards of my private practice, not only in monetary terms, but in terms of personal satisfaction, personal freedom and a sense of accomplishment are such that I have mixed emotions over the possibility of leaving an active trial practice to enter a judicial career." Nevertheless, he asked them to be "considered for a position on the Federal Bench."

He was not just considered; he was nominated by President John F. Kennedy upon the recommendations of Senators Estes Kefauver and Albert Gore. Frank was the fifth district judge appointed by President Kennedy after he took the office of presidency. President Kennedy then nominated three others to Tennessee benches before his assassination in 1963.

For Frank Wilson —
with my best wishes —
John Kennedy

June 1961

The hearing for Frank Wilson was held on June 13, 1961, before the Senate Judiciary subcommittee.

𝔘𝔫𝔦𝔱𝔢𝔡 𝔖𝔱𝔞𝔱𝔢𝔰 𝔖𝔢𝔫𝔞𝔱𝔢

COMMITTEE ON THE JUDICIARY

~~2228~~ NEW SENATE OFFICE BUILDING
2300

SIR:

There will be a HEARING before a subcommittee of the COM-

MITTEE ON THE JUDICIARY on ....Tuesday, June 13, 1961..,

at ....10:30 AM...., upon:

.....Nomination of FRANK W. WILSON, of Tennessee,....

....to be U. S. district judge, eastern district....

...of Tennessee....

BY ORDER OF THE CHAIRMAN   63653-h   GPO

When Frank Wilson was nominated, Senator Al Gore Sr. wrote him: "This is one of the happiest events of my entire public career." On the day of his confirmation in room 2300 of the New Senate Office Building, his onetime opponent, Congressman Howard Baker, testified before the Senate Judiciary Committee, "I recommend him without hesitation and with complete confidence."

Thus, on June 14, 1961, at 10:55 a.m., Frank Wiley Wilson was confirmed by the United States Senate as the United States District Judge for the Eastern District of Tennessee.

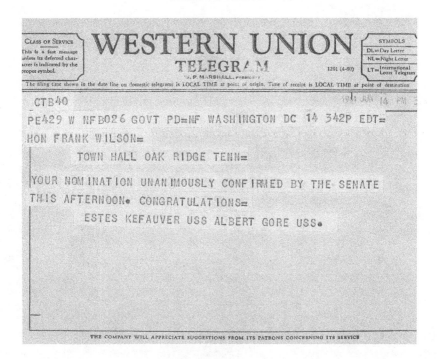

There were two divisions of the Eastern District of Tennessee at that time: the Eastern (in Chattanooga and Winchester) and the Northern (in Knoxville and Greenville). There were two federal judges in the two divisions, one in Chattanooga and one in Knoxville; today, there are six, two in Chattanooga, three in Knoxville, and one in Greenville.

Judge Wilson held the position of federal judge and then chief judge of the Eastern District of Tennessee until September 29, 1982, when he died at his kitchen table revising a jury charge for the next day. There may have been a number of factors contributing to his early demise at age sixty-five: the Hoffa trial and the Mapp trial, both of which will be visited, as well as the statistic that he shared often with others—that the ratio of the number of cases settled to the number of cases filed in the Eastern District of Tennessee was the lowest of all districts in the United States, making his district the most litigious district in the country.

When he became chief judge of the Eastern District of Tennessee, he and Helen were invited by President Gerald Ford to dinner at the White House in November 1975.

The President and Mrs. Ford

request the pleasure of the company of

Chief Judge and Mrs. Wilson

at dinner

on Monday, November 24, 1975

at eight o'clock

ck Tie

DINNER

Ste. Michelle
Semillon
1971

Coquille of Shrimp
Cheese Sticks

Robert Mondavi
Cabernet
Sauvignon
1971

Broiled Châteaubriand
Sauce Béarnaise
Braised Celery
Sweet Peas with Pearl Onions

Beaulieu
Extra Dry
1970

Bibb Lettuce
Cheddar Cheese

Raspberry Ice

THE WHITE HOUSE
Monday, November 24, 1975

During his career, he twice turned down the opportunity of serving on the Sixth Circuit Court of Appeals and was also interviewed as a possible Supreme Court nominee. Frank Wilson preferred being a trial judge, however. As a trial judge, he dealt with people and their problems and witnessed the raw emotion that was visible from the trial bench. As a trial judge, he worked with juries, instructing them on the law and guiding them through their deliberations. He saw the intensity with which jurors performed their task of deciding cases. He also had a close working relationship with the lawyers who appeared before him, learning whom to or whom not to trust. If he had chosen to be an appellate judge, he would have had to give that up and consider his cases solely upon the papers—briefs and transcripts—that were presented to the court.

Frank was inducted on July 1, 1961. Following his confirmation, the congratulatory letters flooded in from across the globe. The *Chattanooga Times* reported that Senator Estes Kefauver was among the spectators in the jury box in the courtroom over which he was soon to preside. He was sworn in beneath a famous mural depicting the history of the Tennessee Valley located in the main courtroom of the Federal Building on floor 3.

His own notes of the sequence of the induction events started with his scripture preference, which was a reading from Deuteronomy 1:1–17, with Moses saying to the children of Israel:

> And I charge you judges at that time, saying, Hear the causes between your brethren, and judge righteously between every man and his brother, and the stranger that is with him.

It was the end of his remarks that showed a new beginning for the conduct of trials before him, treating everyone—parties and attorneys—with dignity and courtesy:

> I fully recognize considerable authority and some immunity—such as tenure—are granted to District Judges. I am further keenly aware of the fact that authority does not become some persons. From practice as a trial lawyer for the

> past twenty years, I have known judges who gave wise and
> just decisions but who used their position and authority to
> make life unpleasant and difficult for most who came in
> contact with them—particularly lawyers practicing in their
> courts. Authority did not become them. A federal judge
> is given considerable authority and immunities—when
> humbly, kindly, and gracefully used you are hardly aware
> of their existence—you just know that justice seems to be
> achieved in an agreeable manner. I hope that the lawyers and
> others who come in contact with this court will find it an
> agreeable place to work and practice your profession.

His humility never wavered, and his gracious treatment, not only of all the lawyers who appeared before him but also of the litigants, was well-known. He dispensed justice humbly, kindly, and gracefully, hardly ever raising his voice, even if provoked. In the twenty-one years he presided, he never developed the judicial disease known as robitis or black robe fever, both of which are symptomized by supremacy of ego and pomposity when donning judicial robes.

The day he was sworn in, he appointed Helen Gannaway from the firm of Spears, Moore, Rebman & Williams as his secretary and John Hennis as his law clerk. Bruce Guthrie was then sworn in as Assistant US Attorney of the Eastern District of Tennessee.

The span of time between his swearing in and his first significant case was short. Judge Frank Wilson was given his test of fire in the case of *United States v. James R. Hoffa Jr*. Before that famous case is reviewed in detail, it bears mention that Frank Wilson almost left the bench as fast as he got to it. In 1963, he was mentioned as a front-runner in the US Senate race to replace Senator Estes Kefauver after his death. Thankfully, in August of 1963, he declined, only to face a bigger challenge in January 1964 with Jimmy Hoffa.

He also had a few light moments before that case, celebrating his first year on the bench with his sons, Frank and Randy:

And Randy, although young at the time, perceived the hard work of his father when he wrote to President Lyndon Johnson.

103 Stratford Way
Signal Mountain
Tennssee
        37377

Dear President Johnson,
    I am the son of Judge Frank W. Wilson,I am writing this letter
to seeif you would or could apoint another Federal Judge to help
my father.He stays up very late at night and sometimes into the
morning working on things in court.I sure hope you do.I live in
Chattanooga Tennssee.

                              Your friend,
                              Randy Wilson

CHAPTER FOUR

Hoffa!

You stand here convicted of seeking to corrupt the administration of justice itself. You stand here convicted having tampered, really, with the very soul of this nation. You stand here convicted of having struck at the very foundation upon which everything else in this nation depends, the basis of civilization itself, and that is the administration of justice, because without a fair, proper and lawful administration of justice, nothing else would be possible in the country.

—Judge Frank Wilson
on the sentencing of James R. Hoffa

Before the Hoffa trial is discussed and in order to help put it in perspective, it may be illustrative to describe briefly what a jury trial is all about. First, the right to a jury trial is a constitutionally protected right, both in the Federal Constitution and in the constitutions of the various states. It is the jury that determines what the facts are and, in criminal trials, whether the accused is guilty. A jury trial itself is a miracle if you consider that twelve people (in most jury trials) who do not know one another are asked to hear facts (evidence) in a way they are not accustomed to hearing facts (through live witnesses and documents). They then hear the arguments of the lawyers and the instructions on the law from a judge and then retire to deliberate in a closed room, where these twelve who do not know one another reach a unanimous verdict—nothing shy of a miracle.

The role of the judge in a jury trial is that of a gatekeeper or referee—mainly in terms of deciding which evidence will be heard by the jury. In the trial of James R. Hoffa, this was a contentious proposition, mainly in terms of whether the evidence proffered by either side was relevant. Relevant evidence, which is determined by the judge, is that evidence that more likely than not tends to prove or disprove a disputed issue of fact.

Usually, a jury trial is tried by lawyers who are acting as effective advocates for their clients but who also try the case within the bounds of civility and the rules. Unfortunately, there are exceptions to this rule. If the lawyers for one side believe, for one reason or another, that the jury will not be able to reach a verdict for their client, they may intentionally try to force the judge into making an error so that they can obtain a reversal of the jury's verdict on appeal. With a patient judge, the lawyers may have to resort to baiting the judge into making that error. And that was what happened in the trial of James R. Hoffa, on a scale that was unprecedented.

In 1964, the then chief of the International Brotherhood of Teamsters Union, Jimmy Hoffa, arrived in Chattanooga, Tennessee, to stand trial for tampering with a jury. That jury had been unable to reach a verdict in a federal criminal trial held the year before in Nashville, Tennessee. A mistrial had been declared on December 23, 1962, after forty-two days of testimony and over seventeen hours of deliberation. This case was the third time that Hoffa had been on the defense, in cases in which the Attorney General of the United States had sought convictions, and Hoffa had survived all three. These three attempts had culminated in the creation of the Get Hoffa Squad in the Office of the Attorney General of the United States—Robert F. Kennedy.

The case in Nashville was presided over by Judge William Miller, who commented after the mistrial was declared that he had been greatly disturbed by reports during the trial that jurors had been improperly approached. Eleven months later, it was discovered that Hoffa's local counsel in that trial, Tommy Osborn, had attempted to tamper with that jury. After a confrontational hearing in chambers with Judge Miller, Osborn was found to have made the attempt and was disbarred. The irony is that Osborn had just previously been inducted into the prestigious American College of Trial Lawyers and was slated to be the president of the Nashville Bar Association. After protracted hearings, Osborn was required to surrender his law license, after which he committed suicide.

When the indictment against Hoffa and others was returned in the Middle District of Tennessee, both judges recused themselves as having been involved with the trials that led to the indictment. A search for a new judge to try the defendants was initiated. The result was the newly installed judge for the Eastern District of Tennessee, Frank Wiley Wilson.

Hoffa's defense to the charge of tampering with that jury was that he didn't know about it, but if he did know about it, he didn't do it. Someone else must have done it for him. So to deal with Hoffa's defense, the government set out to prove not only that he knew about it but also that he orchestrated it—that he sent his underlings, Allen Dorfman, Ewing King, Larry Campbell, Thomas Parks, and Nicholas Tweel, to do it. The government focused upon the attempts to turn two jurors from the Nashville case: Gordon Fields and Betty Paschal.

In arguing cases to a jury in the 1960s, it was often customary to quote scripture in closing arguments, and Jim Neal, the young Assistant US Attorney who tried Hoffa, together with John J. Hooker, did just that. At the end of a seven-week trial, and in response to Hoffa's argument, Neal, in his closing to the jury, paraphrased the biblical story of Jacob and Esau. In that story, Jacob covered his hands with animal hair, pretending to be his brother, Esau, and fooled his blind father into giving him Esau's birthright. Neal's voice rang out, deriding Hoffa's defense that he didn't do it by likening him to Jacob, "The hands may have been the hands of Campbell, Parks, Dorfman, Tweel, and King, but the voice was the voice of Hoffffaaaa." The jury of twelve unanimously found Hoffa and three of his five codefendants guilty.

Besides Hoffa, the defendants were Ewing King of Nashville, a former Teamster local president who was represented by Chattanooga attorney Harold Brown; Allen Dorfman, a close friend of Hoffa who was a Chicago insurance broker who handled insurance for the union and represented by Illinois attorney Harvey Silets; Larry Campbell of Inkster, Michigan, a business agent for Detroit Local 299 and who was represented by Nashville attorney Cecil Branstetter; Thomas Parks of Nashville, who was represented by New York attorney Jacques Schiffer; and Parks's uncle, Nicholas J. Tweel of Huntsville, West Virginia, president of Tobacco and Continental Insurance Company, who was represented by Nashville attorney Dave Alexander and Chattanooga attorney Henry Grady. Representing Hoffa were attorneys James E. Haggerty and Chattanooga attorneys Harry Berke and his son Marvin Berke. In addition to the fact that the case was a high-profile national case, Judge Wilson was faced with the additional problem that of the nine attorneys representing the defendants and the three attorneys representing the United States, only three were from Chattanooga. A trial judge is faced with a number of problems in trying a complex case—staying focused on the issues, controlling the pace and progress of the case, making rulings on the admissibility of evidence, ruling on motions as they arise, and dealing with the needs of the jury and witnesses. But in making these decisions, he must also know about the attorneys—who can he believe with respect to the statements made to the court, who is giving him an accurate representation as to what the law is and who is stretching it, and who is trying to get him to make a mistake. In short, a trial judge must know whom he can trust, and credibility with the court is uppermost in the minds of most attorneys—unless you aren't going to practice in front of this judge again.

Before the Hoffa case started, the defense started with its motions—motions to delay the trial, the need for more time to prepare, the need for time for publicity to settle down, and others, all of which Judge Wilson denied. Motions were even made to the number of FBI agents and court marshals brought in for the case—at least thirty, most of whom were from Detroit—with the attorneys for the defendants arguing that the number of marshals made it look like they were guilty.

On that point, the attorneys argued before, during, and after the trial that they were constantly surveilled by the FBI, making it difficult for them to represent their clients. Finally, a motion was made even as to the layout of the courtroom, with one defendant's counsel arguing that it was too crowded and that he was able to see some jurors only from their chest up. This brought one of the few humorous comments from Judge Wilson during the trial when he asked what further portion of the juror's anatomy he needed to see.

When Hoffa arrived before the trial started on January 21, 1964, he was greeted by enthusiastic crowds both at the Chattanooga Airport and at meetings of various clubs in Chattanooga. But later, on February 9, after the trial was in full swing, a rally at the Tivoli Theater brought only two hundred to three hundred people.

After all the preliminary proceedings, the trial began in the main courtroom on the third floor of the Joel W. Solomon Federal Building in downtown Chattanooga on Tuesday, January 21, 1964. The courtroom is one with extremely high ceilings, two main doors, two side doors, and two end doors, with a door in the wall directly behind the bench through which Judge Wilson entered. Over the judge's chair hangs the sword of Damocles and a mural of the history of the Tennessee Valley from Civil War times through the 1940s. The jury box and the witness stand are on the front right of the courtroom as one enters it—to the left of the judge.

The trial began that Tuesday with jury selection, and the court adjourned at 4:00 p.m. without the selection of a single juror. The voir dire or jury selection phase is usually conducted by the lawyers who try to determine through their questions whether the juror's beliefs will favor his client or the opposing side. If the belief is strong enough to become biased, the juror will be excused for cause, but if not, the attorney may excuse the juror for no reason other than the belief the juror is biased. This challenge is known as a peremptory challenge, and each side has a limited number. Argument was even held over the number of peremptory challenges for each side.

From a defense standpoint, the objective in selecting a jury is to seat twelve jurors who most closely resemble the client. If defense counsel are unable to do this, or even if it can be done, the next step is to create reversible error in case the jury ultimately finds the defendant guilty. Reversible error is created when the court makes erroneous rulings during the trial. One way to create this type of error is to try the judge, not just the case. Thus, counsel will either object to evidence rulings to try to create that error or, in rare occasions, try to bait the judge into making them. And this case was no exception, and it even reached new limits. It is rare to see a case where counsel is held in criminal contempt of court, but this case was an exception. Some counsel were not only combative, but they were also extremely disrespectful, to such a degree that Judge Wilson held one in criminal contempt of court at the end of the trial and sentenced him to jail.

Selection of the jury proceeded into Wednesday, but on Wednesday, Judge Wilson began to become impatient with the amount of time it was taking to select the jury. He told the lawyers, "Unless voir dire is considerably more expeditiously handled, the court will take over the voir dire."

On Wednesday, January 22, Judge Wilson did just that; he took over voir dire of the jury that morning. He explained his thoughts:

> I have reflected overnight upon the progress being made in the selection of the jury in this case. In two days, we have as yet not selected as single juror to try this case. We have completed the *voir dire* examination upon only six prospective jurors. If all challenges for favor are exercised, it would be necessary to complete an additional thirty *voir dire*. At the rate we have been progressing, this would require approximately three weeks to select a jury.

Not only was the process slowed by the exercise of the normal challenges, but more importantly, he felt the process was being slowed by unnecessary questioning:

> The result has been to so slow the progress of the trial with matters not appropriate to a *voir dire* examination that we stand today without a single juror selected. Among the six

upon whom *voir dire* has been completed, not a single one was completed within an hour, and several ran considerably over an hour in length.

And so he explained, change would be necessary:

This court, if it is to administer justice, must function within reasonable dispatch. Procedures which prevent the court from functioning must not be allowed to continue.

I have therefore concluded, gentlemen, that the procedures for conducting *voir dire* must be modified and that the court should take over the *voir dire* examination in accordance with Rule 24(a).

The examination of a single juror at a time will be discontinued. A sufficient number of jurors to complete the panel with alternates will be examined at one time. The examination will be by the court.

Not only were the difficulties encountered in the selection of the panel of jurors from the pool of jurors summoned to serve, but objections were also raised by defense counsel to the ultimate composition of the panel. The jurors from which the attorneys select a jury are generally selected from the public at large using a variety of sources of information, such as tax rolls, voter registrations, and utility bills. In this case, however, the objection came *two weeks after the jury pool had actually been selected* and did not question the way in which the pool had been selected. The objection, which was often repeated during the trial, was that the jury was not representative of a cross section of Chattanooga. Judge Wilson, however, ruled that the objection not only was made too late but was also made to the particular jury as selected, not from the pool from which they were chosen.

After four days of the selection process from January 21 to January 24, the jury was seated and sworn. The jury consisted of eight men and four women, only one of whom was African American.

Judge Wilson started the first day of testimony on Monday, January 27, with instructions to the attorneys as well as to the jury. Some of these instructions would be repeated on a regular basis during the trial because they were simply disregarded by the lawyers: "Instruct counsel about no improper argument before jury—for example, talk of jury custody—or court will deal severely with any deliberate argument, not tolerate clear violations of this instruction."

He also instructed the jury:

> Ladies and gentlemen, the court would like, at this time, to explain to you very briefly the nature of the case that you are about to hear.
>
> First Count, the indictment in this case originally contained five counts. The first of these counts is not for trial at this time. However, you will therefore be concerned with only counts two, three, four, and five.
>
> Counts two to five, these counts involve four alleged violations of title 18, section 1503 of the United States Code, commonly referred to as the Federal Obstruction of Justice Statute.
>
> Statute, this statute provides, in relevant part, that "whoever corruptly...endeavors to influence, intimidate, or impede any...petit juror...in the discharge of his duty...or corruptly...endeavors to influence, obstruct, or impede the due administration of justice, shall be" punished as provided by law.

He then explained that Hoffa was the only one who had been indicted on all counts, two through five. He explained that Hoffa, Campbell, and Parks were indicted on count 3 for attempting to influence juror Gratin Fields through his son, Carl. Under count 4, Hoffa, Tweel, and Dorfman were indicted for attempting to influence Dallas Hall to get to other jurors. Finally, under count 5, Hoffa and King were indicted for attempting to influence juror Betty Paschal through her husband. The jury returned its verdict, and guilt was found under counts 2, 3, and 5 but not 4. Hoffa, Campbell, and Parks were found guilty of "endeavoring to influence Mr. Fields, and King and Hoffa were found guilty of endeavoring to influence Ms. Paschal." Tweel, Hoffa, and Dorfman were found not guilty of obstruction of justice in an alleged attempt to influence Dallas Hall.

Before the testimony started on that Monday, defense counsel had asked that the jury be sequestered so that they would not be exposed to publicity during the trial. Judge Wilson agreed but was immediately tested when the defendants did a complete about-face and complained that the jury should not have been sequestered. Judge Wilson felt that such an argument could only be taken as an apparent attempt to create error, and he commented on the defense tactics, saying, "Throughout the history of this lawsuit, the defendants have complained repeatedly and most vehemently of the alleged adverse effects of publicity upon their obtaining a fair trial. Each day last week, a new motion in this respect was made. Now when the court takes steps to remove the jury from any possible influence by publicity by having them remain together and supervising their access to publicity, thereby assuring a trial upon evidence heard in open court, defendants complain equally vehemently and frequently of this action of the court. It was the control of publicity on any influence outside the courtroom in mind that this court felt it appropriate and in the interest of a fair trial that the jury be held together. The court must perform its function as it sees its duty and does not have available to it the luxury of being inconsistent." This was the first example of "trying the judge" instead of trying the case.

After the court dealt with preliminary matters, the government then started the presentation of its case, consisting of thirty-eight witnesses. Thirteen testified during the first week of trial that various telephone calls were made to and from the defendants in various locations, most of which either originated from or were made to telephone numbers in Nashville and to or from the telephone numbers of the defendants or places frequented by the defendants. Thus, in the first week, the government succeeded in showing that the defendants were only talking among themselves. Although a great deal of evidence was received about the fact that the calls were made, there was little, if any, testimony about what was said.

There were also witnesses who testified about access to the jurors who were the focus of the government's case: Mrs. Paschal and Mr. Fields. Five FBI agents had followed the defendant King in connection with meetings he had with the state trooper husband of Betty Paschal. Other witnesses included the son and daughter of Gratin Fields, who had been contacted by Campbell and Parks. Of interest was that there was never any testimony that either the children of Juror Fields actually talked with their father about the case or that Trooper Paschal ever talked with his wife about the case. But attempts were shown.

The government's case lasted from Monday, January 27, to Friday, February 14. Just a side observation of the intensity with which Judge Wilson tried this case, Judge Wilson's son, Randy, remembered his father rarely went to bed before 3:00 a.m., pouring over the daily transcripts that were delivered to his house by 7:00 p.m. each evening.

The proof that began on that Monday, January 27, started with the testimony of James T. Walker, an officer with the Nashville Metro police. Walker testified that he was a neighbor of Gordon Fields and was approached by Defendant Parks. He said Parks asked him if Fields needed money and that Parks told him that "the big boys" wanted to talk to Fields because they only needed one juror to hang the jury to obtain a mistrial. After this conversation between Walker and Parks, Walker testified that he then arranged for a meeting between Parks and Fields's son, Carl. Walker also said Parks asked who the boss of the Fields family was, and when Walker said it was Carl Fields's sister, Mattie, Parks asked him to arrange for him to talk with her also. After meeting with Mattie, Walker said Parks took him home and told him he wanted to take care of him financially, but no amount was mentioned. The jury was adjourned for the day.

On the next day, January 28, Walker's testimony concluded and Carl Fields, the son of Gordon Fields, testified that Walker had called him to talk about his father as a juror in the Hoffa trial. At the first meeting at Walker's house, nothing happened. Carl testified he then met with Walker in Parks's car, and Parks told him that Bobby Kennedy was out to get Hoffa and that he needed him to talk with his father to help out Hoffa. He testified that when Parks offered him $5,000, he said his father would not go for that.

After Carl Fields testified, his sister, Mattie Keith, still living with her father, Gordon, testified. She said she received a call from Jack Walker, who wanted to talk. She said Walker wanted to know what her father was wearing each morning of the trial and if her father needed work. She said she wanted no part of the discussion because she didn't want to mess with the government.

Testimony proceeded tediously on Wednesday, January 29. The telephone witnesses started and identified telephone calls made to or by some of the defendants. By the close of the day on January 29, over forty exhibits had been marked, most of which were records of telephone calls. The trial went back and forth on who telephoned whom, when, and where, but there was no real testimony about what was said in the calls.

By Friday, January 31, most of the testimony other than testimony about Fields was given by witnesses who testified about two matters: that Tweel, Dorfman, or Campbell either made telephone calls to or from Nashville at the time of the Hoffa trial or were in Nashville at the time of the trial in the presence of one another, but other than that, nothing. In other words, by the end of this week, the government showed that these three defendants had the opportunity to accomplish what they were indicted for, not that they had accomplished it.

Monday started the next week with the government focusing on the attempts of the defendants to influence Betty Paschal. Tennessee state trooper James Paschal, husband of juror Betty, took the stand. Although attempts were made by King to get Trooper Paschal to influence his wife through hints at offers of promotion, nothing really incriminating resulted from his testimony, although he was the talk of internal discussions in the Hoffa camp about whether he could be bribed to influence his wife.

But then came Tuesday, February 4, and the government's surprise witness, the man to convict Hoffa—Edward Grady Partin. He was to take the stand after lunch Tuesday, but during the noon recess, some theatrics took place. The *Chattanooga Times* reported that "Hooker [the assistant U. S. Attorney] strode through the corridor with an air of confidence, hinting to newsmen that important events were imminent, but he didn't say exactly what the prosecution was up to." The newspaper report continued, "The Baton Rouge Teamsters union official Tuesday rocked the defense when he appeared as a surprise witness for the Department of Justice." The paper reported that this announcement touched off a "bitter four-hour legal battle." That battle did not last just four hours. It lasted for the rest of the trial with some very vicious attacks on the integrity of Partin and of Judge Wilson.

Partin was in the inner circle of the union. He was the secretary-treasurer of Teamsters Local #5 in Baton Rouge and knew Hoffa, King, Tweel, and Dorfman. He had known Hoffa since 1957 and had dealt with him on both union and personal matters.

When Partin entered the courtroom, the defense had no idea that he was going to testify for the government. And their reaction perhaps showed more to the jury than his testimony. All the poker faces left, and the counsel table was in disarray. Partin had been with Hoffa during the trial in Nashville and had even taken the fifth in front of the grand jury. But now he was in Chattanooga to testify against Hoffa. Apparently, the rift had developed as a result of a disagreement between the two over whether to continue a strike in Baton Rouge, where Partin had been head of the local union. When he volunteered to assist the government, he was, obviously, greeted with skepticism and given a polygraph, which he passed. Until Partin testified, there was a substantial question about whether the government had proved its case and, hence, why all the untoward conduct by Schiffer had been necessary. After Partin's testimony, the contemptuous conduct of Schiffer toward Neal and Judge Wilson intensified.

Partin started his testimony by telling the jury that he had talked with Hoffa two or three days before he came to Nashville and arranged to meet with him there, but while there, he was also going to meet with Frank Grimsby, a government agent. He related that after registering at the Andrew Jackson Hotel in Nashville, he went to Hoffa's room and met with King and Tweel and said he had gotten a call from Allen

Dorfman, asking for a personal favor—come up with a method to get to the Nashville jury.

At this point, defense counsel exploded. They objected that Partin was working as an undercover government agent and was improperly listening in on the advice being given by Hoffa's lawyers. Jim Neal immediately responded that even if he had heard the advice from the lawyers, that advice had been given in the Nashville case, not the Chattanooga case. And even if he heard any such advice, which he denied, it was never used in the Nashville case to Hoffa's detriment. At this point, the jury was excused, and arguments were heard.

When Partin resumed his testimony, he testified that he had heard no advice given and did not even know some of the people in the Nashville trial were lawyers. Nor did he even recall the tactics in the Nashville case being discussed. He also said he was reporting only to agents Sheridan or Grimsby on attempts by Hoffa to tamper with the Nashville jury, not on the trial itself.

Then a parade of lawyers took the stand—all out of the presence of the jury—to hear whether Partin had been unfairly privy to their discussions with Hoffa during the Nashville trial and, thus, whether his testimony could continue. The wagon train started with Attorney Bufalino, who said he talked with Partin several times about strategy; continued with James Haggerty, who also testified Partin was present at the conference table when strategy was being discussed; then Jacob Kossman, who said he saw Partin on many occasions in Hoffa's room; next, David Pendl, who saw Partin in the conference rooms; and finally, Morris Shenker. Testimony was even heard from Walter Sheridan, the special agent, who said Partin was only to report evidence regarding jury tampering by Hoffa and his team in the Nashville trial, not on the merits of the trial itself. Sheridan said Partin gave him no statements made by Hoffa to his attorneys in connection with the merits of the Nashville trial. The argument about whether Partin would be permitted to continue his testimony went over to the next day, February 5, when Judge Wilson made the following findings before the jury was brought back:

1. Overrule motion to suppress testimony of Witness Partin, among other matters

    (a) I find that there has been no interference by the witness with the attorney client relationship of any defendant in this case at any time

    (b) The Government did not place this witness in the Defendants midst or have anything to do with placing him in their midst. Rather he was knowingly and voluntarily placed in their midst by one of the defendants

    (c) As this court understands and interprets the law there is no basis for denying the Government the use of this witness' testimony in this case

    (d) There is no information in the notes and papers of the witness Sheridan that would be proper or lawful to make available to the Defendants

    (e) The request of the Defendants for examination of all FBI reports should be denied.

When the Chattanooga conviction was appealed to the Sixth Circuit Court of Appeals and later to the United States Supreme Court, both courts agreed with Judge Wilson's findings.

Having lost the motion, the defendants tried again with yet another attorney witness, who testified not about the strategy to be used in the Nashville case but about Partin's involvement in voir dire and strategy and jury selection in the Nashville case—to no avail. Judge Wilson let Partin's story be heard by the jury.

After all the parrying back and forth among the lawyers, Partin returned to the stand and testified that on the first day of the trial in Nashville, Tweel called him in to Hoffa's suite and told him they had gotten to one juror but needed to try to get to others. Before he went back to Baton Rouge, Partin testified he talked with Hoffa in his room and that Hoffa told him that when he came back, Hoffa wanted Partin to pass something to a juror for him and hit his rear pocket. At this point in Partin's testimony, the newspaper reported that Schiffer again objected to the testimony and stormed around the courtroom. When Judge Wilson asked if he was through, and when Schiffer said he was, Judge Wilson calmly said, "Overruled." This judge has the patience of Job.

Partin's testimony continued by his telling the jury that he left Nashville for Baton Rouge, but then returned to Nashville. During that stay in Nashville, he brought King into the picture when he said that King told him in the seventh-floor hallway of the hotel that they had gotten to a juror through a highway patrolman (referring to Trooper Paschal, husband of juror Betty Paschal) who loved money and who thought $1,000 was a lot of money. During that stay, Partin said Tweel also gave him a list of jurors to see if there was anyone else on the list they could turn.

Before meeting with King in the seventh-floor hallway, Partin said he had met with Hoffa in his suite, where Hoffa told him that someone had told Judge Miller (presiding in the Nashville trial) what had been going on with attempts to tamper with the jurors. He said that Hoffa said, "The dirty bastards went in and told the judge that his neighbor had offered him $10,000. We are going to have to lay low for a few days," he concluded, and Partin left Nashville again. But then he returned and told of a conversation on Sunday with Hoffa after Hoffa had talked with King that morning. He said Hoffa told him that King was not doing what he was told to do. He said that although King had told him that he had the patrolman, Trooper Paschal, in his pocket, he did not, in fact, have him. Hoffa also told him that he had a "colored male juror in his hip pocket." Hoffa said the juror was a retired railway worker and was their best bet unless they could get to the foreman. He said that a hung jury was as good as acquittal because the government would never try the case again.

Partin then left Nashville again but returned the next afternoon. Hoffa and King were still talking about Trooper Paschal, and he said Hoffa told King he was a "stupid SOB" for not getting his job done. Partin then left for Knoxville, then returned to Nashville again, and said everyone was still discussing Trooper Paschal. After trial adjourned that morning, he saw Hoffa that afternoon, who said things looked pretty good. Partin then left for Dallas for a grievance meeting, returned to

Nashville the following day, and then left for New York, where he got a call from Tweel. He said that Tweel told him things were getting too hot and that the government knew all about the various phone calls that had been testified to using pay phones. He said that Tweel told him that he could not afford to fool with trying to get other jurors and told him to pass the word to get out—that it was too hot.

Schiffer again attacked Judge Wilson for letting Partin testify, accusing him of presiding over a "drum-headed court-martial and a star chamber proceeding." When Judge Wilson told Schiffer to keep his voice down because "the court can hear your remarks without being so loud," Schiffer said, "I will talk up every time." He then continued, "Every time Your Honor sort of bawls me out, the jury sees that." After his tirade, he then sat down.

The frustration of defense counsel in not having been able to score in their cross-examination of Partin was shown in their subsequent attack on Judge Wilson that Friday, which echoed Schiffer's tirade. Schiffer led the charge again. First, he attacked Jim Neal, accusing him of making gestures to inform witnesses how to testify. Then he launched against Judge Wilson, this time making it personal. "I am defending this man on his constitutional rights here, and they are not going to still my tongue if I have to drop dead at this trial, and I mean it." He continued, complaining about Neal and Judge Wilson's conduct of the trial, "I say in deference to Your Honor, if this ever happened in any other federal court, I would have been in jail, and anybody at the prosecution table who counseled and abetted would be in jail. I did not see anybody cautioned here as many times as we seek protection from the court. We don't get it, and every time Your Honor will say something to me in front of this jury, it prejudices Parks." At one point, Judge Wilson asked the court reporter to mark Schiffer's comments on her notes and said, "We will take it up at a later time." That later time was a finding of criminal contempt at the conclusion of the trial.

Argument about Partin's testimony continued Monday, February 10, with objections overruled, and Partin retook the stand and was cross-examined for the entire day. When Partin left the stand, he had endured seven days of testimony, most of which was under cross-examination.

Some observed that had defense counsel ended its cross-examination when Harry Berke concluded his cross-examination, the government's case would have been hurt, but with the continuation, Partin was able to regain ground that he had lost under Berke's cross. There was an observation that Judge Wilson would make in many trials after the Hoffa trial about cross-examination—"If you have a point to make upon cross-examination, make it and sit down." His belief was that if the attorney on cross-examination droned on and on about non-key points, the jury would get lost, and so would his main points.

The defense made another mistake with Partin when they called the doctor who had examined Partin. The defendants had contended that the jury should not believe Partin because he was a drug addict. The doctor testified unequivocally that he had seen no signs of drug addiction in Partin.

The government rested on Friday, February 14, at 11:00 a.m. The case proceeded with the testimony of defendants Tweel, Dorfman, and Parks, who basically testified that they didn't know one another or had any connection with any alleged jury tampering.

Wednesday, February 19, was one of the stormiest days of the trial. The day started with defense offering the testimony of Frederick Michael Shobe to show that Robert Kennedy was an archfoe of Hoffa and that Kennedy was out to get him. His testimony was heard out of the presence of the jury, and when Judge Wilson said he would make a ruling on it later that afternoon, Schiffer objected, arguing that it would interfere with his presentation of the defense.

Out of the presence of the jury, Judge Wilson heard the testimony of the witness Shobe and "even declined to allow prosecution attorneys to interfere with Schiffer's direct examination." Shobe testified that the principal objective in the Department of Justice was to get Hoffa and that he was part of Bobby Kennedy's Get Hoffa Squad. He also testified, "Well, preferably, if there was something found that incriminated Mr. Hoffa, well and good." If not, "the feeling in the department was that Mr. Hoffa should be in jail anyway and that we—if we had to resort to unfair tactics—well, that's where a fellow like myself came in at." Shobe's proffered testimony was that the Department of Justice had come up with an elaborate scheme to fake the abduction of Parks, supposedly by Hoffa, and then rescue him to get him to turn on Hoffa.

After the court heard the testimony, Judge Wilson asked Schiffer, "Are you in good faith offering all of this proof of this witness?" Schiffer responded that it was being offered to prove a frame-up by the government's attorney general, Bobby Kennedy, whereupon Judge Wilson asked other defense attorneys whether they were also offering the testimony in good faith; some of the defense started to retreat. Harry Berke, Hoffa's counsel, said that some of it was competent and some of it was not. Branstetter said the same. After defendant King testified, the defense ended with witnesses to try to discredit the reputation of Partin.

In addition to Shobe's testimony, which had been disallowed, Schiffer also attempted to introduce the testimony of Sol Fox, a real estate man in San Juan and a former mine operator in Pennsylvania. The jury was then sent out again, and Schiffer insisted that with this witness, he wanted to prove that Partin was trying to secure ships to carry arms to Fidel Castro. Neal objected, and Judge Wilson agreed that it was simply not relevant to the jury-tampering charge.

Finally, Berke put Hoffa on the stand. He was composed and denied in detail the testimony of the witnesses who had testified against him, mixing explanations of fact with questions of incredulity as to why anyone would assert that he did some of the stupid things he was supposed to have done. He even explained that he could not have even patted his back pocket, as Partin had testified, when he showed that he carried his money in his vest pocket.

Hooker was designated to perform the cross-examination, and although he tried, he could not get Hoffa to explode. Berke did get Judge Wilson to raise his voice, however, when he ventured into an area to which Judge Wilson had ruled he could not go. When he did so, Judge Wilson admonished, "Counsel will not just willfully disobey the orders and instructions of the court." Hoffa was on the stand for three and one-half hours.

At that point, not having succeeded in getting the testimony of Shobe and Fox before the jury, it appeared that the defense might be nearing the end of its proof. Even when the defendants testified, Schiffer had continued to lambaste the government and Judge Wilson. Thus, on the cross-examination of Defendant Tweel by the government, Schiffer exploded:

> How much does this court want the government to be permitted to use against the defendants unconstitutionally? To what point, Your Honor, are we lawyers supposed to appear here in court and make the pretense of defending according to law, when the government pushes the court to such an untenable position that it cannot do justice in face of the Partins? If a man is given a license by this court to come in and testify under oath and lies, what does Your Honor want from counsel for the defendants? How can we go on with this farce of a trial now when Partin's testimony is permitted to stand in the face of its provable falsity, outright perjury?

At the end of the fifth week of trial, the Chattanooga paper correctly reported that Partin was the "only witness offered by the prosecution to link Hoffa's name with the alleged efforts to bribe and otherwise illegally influence a jury, which tried the Teamsters union president on charges of violating the Taft-Hartley labor law in Nashville in 1962." But link him it did.

The jury returned its verdict of guilt against Hoffa and two others on March 3 at 1:58 p.m. Hoffa, Parks, and Campbell were found guilty of count 3 of the indictment in which it was alleged they attempted to influence Fields; Tweel, Dorfman, and Hoffa were found not guilty of count 4, the obstruction of justice count; and King and Hoffa were found guilty of count 5, which alleged they attempted to influence Mrs. Paschal.

At the same time that he received the jury's verdict with respect to the defendants, Judge Wilson immediately announced that "a certificate of contempt will be filed in this case after the court has had an opportunity to make an appropriate review of the record." That certificate of contempt would be lodged against Schiffer.

At his sentencing, Hoffa continued to protest that he was innocent and "that ultimately when the evidence has been sifted calmly, coolly, and collectively…I will be found innocent." There was no acceptance of the verdict, no plea for clemency, no expression of remorse—just defiance.

Judge Wilson responded in a sentencing statement that was printed around the United States. In that statement, Judge Wilson did not just sentence an individual for the crime for which he was convicted. He sentenced him for a crime against society, for an attack by Hoffa on the very principles by which a free society is governed, when he said this:

> Now it is difficult for the court to imagine under those circumstances a more willful violation of the law. The defendants that stand before this court for sentencing, and certainly sentencing is the most distressing duty that this court ever has to perform. Most defendants that stand before this court for sentencing have either violated the property rights of other individuals or have violated the personal rights of other individuals.

> You stand here convicted of seeking to corrupt the administration of justice itself. You stand here convicted of having tampered, really, with the very soul of this nation. You stand here convicted of having struck at the very foundation upon which everything else in this nation depends, the basis of civilization itself, and that is the administration of justice because without a fair, proper, and lawful administration of justice, nothing else would be possible in the country, the administration of labor unions, the administration of business, the carrying on of occupations, the carrying on of recreation, the administration of health services. Everything that we call civilization depends ultimately upon the proper administration of justice itself.

> Now if a conviction of such an offense were to not be punished and this type of conduct permitted to pass without action by this court, it would surely destroy this country more quickly and more surely than any combination of foreign foes ever hoped to do.

Sentence was then pronounced against Hoffa—on the two counts on which he was convicted: four years in prison for each count and a fine of $5,000 on each count, with the sentences to run consecutively, not concurrently. When asked if he understood the sentence, Hoffa responded, "I understand the sentence perfectly, and I will take my appeals." Campbell, Parks, and King were each sentenced to three years. After he was sentenced, Hoffa turned from the bench to leave, but the US Marshal approached him and asked him to extend his hands. Berke said to the Marshal that he was on bail, whereupon Judge Wilson said that he was not, that he had just remanded Mr. Hoffa to the custody of the United States Marshal, who then handcuffed him and took him away. Hoffa had previously told that Marshal, Harry Mansfield, "Harry, I can shut this country down with one phone call."

James R. Hoffa was then taken to a Hamilton County jail cell approximately two and a half blocks up the hill from the federal courthouse and across from the Hamilton County Courthouse.

But the sentencing of Hoffa was not the only sentencing Judge Wilson was to perform at the end of the trial. More pages of transcript were consumed in finding Jacques M. Schiffer, counsel, not for Hoffa but for Thomas Ewing Parks, in criminal contempt for a "deliberate and willful attack upon the administration of justice," "an attempt to prevent by improper means the functioning of this court," "an attempt to debase and degrade this court," and "such misconduct...as would be calculated to destroy all respect for this court...if such conduct went unnoticed and unpunished by this court." There followed over thirteen pages of examples of contemptuous conduct committed by Schiffer over the course of the trial, and it should be remembered that Schiffer was not even Hoffa's lawyer. Perhaps, however, he was elected to be a stalking horse.

After the jury returned its verdict and Hoffa was sentenced, Hoffa's team not only asked for a new trial but also asked Judge Wilson to disqualify himself as the trial judge. That motion came eighteen months after the jury reported its verdict and after Hoffa's conviction had been affirmed on appeal by the Sixth Circuit Court of Appeals. To support their motion, which attorneys who file the motion are required to sign, but which the local attorneys for Hoffa refused to sign, the defendants submitted the affidavit of a prostitute who swore that Judge Wilson and some of the jurors visited her at the Read House, where the jurors had been sequestered during the trial. The motion was denied, and the affidavit was found to be a "complete and total fabrication and fraud." In ruling on the motion to disqualify, Judge Wilson wrote, "There is as much obligation upon a judge not to recuse himself when there is no occasion as there is for him to do so when there is cause."

There followed yet another blunderbuss motion for a new trial, decided by Judge Wilson in 1965. In that opinion, Judge Wilson recited history of the case up to the time of trial as follows:

> The defendants were indicted under the federal obstruction of justice statute upon May 9, 1963, and charged with willfully endeavoring to influence, intimidate, and impede jurors in the discharge of their duties. After lengthy proceedings, including two petitions by the defendants to the Court of Appeals for mandamus, each of which petitions was denied, the case went to trial upon January 20, 1964. After seven weeks of trial, the jury returned a verdict of guilty against the defendants, Hoffa, Parks, Campbell, and King, and acquitted two other codefendants. The original motion for new trial, asserting ninety-two grounds, was filed upon March 10, 1964. This motion was overruled by the opinion of the court filed April 8, 1964, and at the time that it was set for argument in the Court of the Appeals, the defendants filed their second motion for new trial, this motion being based upon allegedly newly discovered evidence…This court overruled the second motion for new trial by an opinion filed April 15, 1965, and the appeal is presently pending in the Court of Appeals. In the meantime, the Court of Appeals affirmed the conviction of the defendants upon the initial appeal upon July 29, 1965. Shortly thereafter, the defendants filed the present motion for new trial upon September 1, 1965, being the third such motion filed and the second motion to be based upon allegedly newly discovered evidence.

This was the second motion that asked Judge Wilson to disqualify himself, and he held that the "motion to reconsider raises no matters that were not fully covered in the opinion of this court filed September 22, 1965." The case was not finally resolved, however, until over a year later by the Supreme Court's decision on December 12, 1966. In that decision, the Supreme Court was presented with arguments under the Fourth Amendment (that Partin had conducted an illegal search), the Sixth Amendment (Partin, by eavesdropping, had violated Hoffa's right to counsel), and the Fifth Amendment.

In its decision, the Supreme Court summarily rejected the first two of Hoffa's arguments under the Fourth Amendment and the Fifth Amendment. Under the Fourth Amendment, Hoffa had argued that Partin, as an alleged informer for the government, had conducted an illegal search of his hotel room by listening to the conversations of Hoffa with others, including his lawyers. The court responded by finding no constitutional violation because Hoffa "was not relying on the security of his hotel suite," that Partin did not "enter by force or stealth," and that some of the incriminating statement had even been made by Hoffa to Partin in the public areas of the hotel. In holding Hoffa's claims under the Fifth Amendment to be "without merit," the court held that "no claim has been or could be made that the petitioner's incriminating statements were the product of any sort of coercion, legal or factual."

The Supreme Court then discussed Hoffa's claims under the Sixth Amendment—that his right to counsel had been violated by Partin's eavesdropping. The court rejected this argument, agreeing with what Judge Wilson had previously found, by finding "that none of the petitioner's incriminating statements which Partin heard were made in the presence of counsel." The court also rejected Hoffa's argument under the Sixth Amendment because any intrusion on his right to counsel was in a different case; there simply was no intrusion on his right to counsel in the jury-tampering case.

Lastly, the Supreme Court addressed the argument that while there may have been no violation of the Fourth, Fifth, or Sixth Amendments separately, the due process clause of the Fifth Amendment calls for a reversal of the conviction based upon the "'totality' of the government's conduct." In other words, Hoffa's attorneys argued he had not been dealt with fairly because of the use of Partin. In the words of the Court,

Hoffa argued that the use of informers "is a shabby thing in any case." Although the majority of the court summarily rejected the argument, Justice Warren dissented. In his dissent, Justice Warren relied upon the lack of veracity and the motives of Partin, who was the only evidence that supported the jury's verdict. The majority of the court disagreed with Justice Warren, however, and pointed out that in the system of jurisprudence, "established safeguards of the Anglo-American legal system leave the veracity of a witness to be tested by cross-examination and the credibility of his testimony to be determined by a properly instructed jury." Finding that Partin had been vigorously cross-examined and that the jury was properly instructed, the court concluded that the "Constitution does not require us to upset the jury's verdict."

After the trial, Judge Wilson reached out to J. Edgar Hoover to thank him for the security provided during the trial, which included escorts to and from the courthouse and escorts for his children to and from school. Hoover responded as follows:

JOHN EDGAR HOOVER
DIRECTOR

Federal Bureau of Investigation
United States Department of Justice
Washington, D. C.

April 14, 1964

Honorable Frank W. Wilson
United States District Judge
Chattanooga, Tennessee 37402

My dear Judge:

      I have received your letter of April 9th commenting so favorably on the work of the FBI in connection with the case of James R. Hoffa, et al.

      It was certainly good of you to give me the benefit of your observations regarding the efforts of Special Agents of this Bureau on this investigation. You may be sure my associates appreciate, as I do, your thoughtfulness in writing as you did.

            Sincerely yours,

            J. Edgar Hoover

It should be noted that throughout the trial, defense counsel continuously and bitterly complained that they were being followed everywhere by FBI agents, a contention that was not proved other than by the complaints themselves.

It was not until 1972, six years after the Supreme Court's decision and eight years after the trial, that the case was finally put to rest when Judge Wilson denied the fifth posttrial motion. With everything that he endured during the trial, Judge Wilson survived all attempts of defense counsel to provoke him into error.

CHAPTER FIVE

Four Other Significant Trials

> Quality education might not seem so difficult for anyone to
> maintain if it were truly his brother's child that was being
> deprived or handicapped by its denial.
>
> —Decision, *Mapp v.*
> *City of Chattanooga School Board*

Years after Hoffa, Judge Wilson presided over four other lengthy, difficult,
controversial, and significant trials: *Mapp v. City of Chattanooga School
Board*, *Wiley v. Franklin*, *Tennessee Valley Authority v. Allis-Chalmers*,
and *Weems v. Yeomans*. The first and most significant of these cases was
Mapp, which was pending at the time he took the bench. The case was
filed in 1959, in the wake of the Supreme Court's decision in *Brown v.
Board of Education*.

The opinion in *Brown*, the well-known case that ended segregation
in public schools, was written by Chief Justice Earl Warren. Warren had
been Thomas Dewey's vice presidential running mate against Harry
Truman in 1948. Rather than issuing the opinion of the court in
Brown, with possible dissenting or concurring separate opinions, Chief
Justice Warren held it until the vote of the court was unanimous. As
significant as the decision was, it, obviously, was not well received in

certain portions of the country, and in 1959, one of those areas was Chattanooga, Tennessee. Lead stories by John Popham ran in the *New York Times* and the *Chattanooga Times*, with the *Chattanooga* lead line, "Reactions of the South." Among the reactions reported by Popham was the statement by Georgia governor Herman Talmadge that there "would never be mixed schools while I am governor." Thus, the environment in which *Mapp* was to be decided by Judge Wilson was not, to say the least, one of acceptance.

In the *Mapp* case, James Mapp sought successfully to desegregate the Chattanooga City school system. Judge Wilson received abuse from both sides of the issue for his decisions. For some, he went too far. For others, he did not go far enough. It was an issue on which he could do no right, but the wisdom expressed in those decisions showed that he did, and his decision was ultimately upheld.

The reason for the length of time to resolve the case lay in the ever-changing decisions issued by the federal appellate courts, including the Supreme Court, in a new area of the law. In the course of its twenty-seven-year history, *Mapp* went through at least four trial-level hearings and three appellate decisions.

Judge Wilson's first decision in 1971 started as follows: "This case is presently before the court for settlement upon a plan that will accomplish full and final desegregation of the Chattanooga, Tennessee, public schools in accordance with recent decisions of the United States Supreme Court and of the United States Court of Appeals for this Circuit." He then recited the history of the case, which had included numerous prior hearings and which concluded with a hearing on May 19, 1971. In issuing his decision, Judge Wilson very carefully laid out what he felt the role of the court was in reviewing the plans proposed by the Chattanooga Board of Education. He believed that it was not his function to judge whether he agreed with the plan but to "leave to the school board the maximum discretion and responsibility for all phases of the city's plan of operation of the Chattanooga public schools, limited only by constitutional requirements. Absent a constitutional violation, the wisdom or lack of wisdom of any plan or policy established by the board is not a proper subject for judicial intervention or direction. The court should not substitute its judgment for that of the school board in areas where the exercise of judgment does not violate some principle of the law." Thus, Judge Wilson clearly established the principle by which the city's plan of desegregation was to be reviewed. The function of the judiciary was not to decide whether or not the city's plan was a good one but rather to limit its review to whether the plan comported with the principles of the Fourteenth Amendment of the Constitution of the United States. In walking that narrow line between upholding the board's plan and finding it unconstitutional, Judge Wilson approved the plan, and his approval of the plan was affirmed by the Court of Appeals. That, you might think, was the end of the dispute, but while the case was on appeal, another decision of the United States Supreme Court intervened, and *Mapp* was sent back to Judge Wilson for reconsideration in light of that decision. That new issue focused on whether there had been segregation of teachers and not just students. That issue had arisen in a case in Charlotte, North Carolina, after Judge Wilson's approval of the Chattanooga plan but before the Sixth Circuit Court of Appeals had considered it. So the Sixth Circuit had to send the case back to Judge Wilson for further consideration. In considering that issue on remand, Judge Wilson found that the assignment of personnel on a racial basis was unconstitutional without the necessity of showing an adverse effect on the education of students because such an assignment "impairs the students' rights to an education free of any consideration of race." His finding was almost as if Judge Wilson had anticipated the argument. He then gave the school board an opportunity to submit a plan to rid the system of any vestiges of segregation in school personnel.

In considering the plan, which had been submitted, Judge Wilson recited the history of the *Mapp* litigation, which had commenced in the late fifties. One of the attorneys who had originally filed the suit, Constance Baker Motley, went on to become a federal judge in the Southern District of New York. Judge Wilson described that history: "Following appellate guidelines as they then existed, this court believed upon each previous occasion it entered desegregation orders, first in 1962, then in 1965 and 1967, that all vestiges of the dual system of schools would be removed upon fulfillment of its orders and only a unitary system remain. Experience and appellate redefinition of the concept of a unitary school system have now mandated that further steps be taken to accomplish the full and final desegregation of the Chattanooga schools. As reflected by the undisputed evidence, a number of the Chattanooga schools remain racially identifiable." By the phrase, *racially identifiable*, he meant segregated. Judge Wilson found that the board's plan under consideration provided for "no school having less than 30 percent nor more than 70 percent of one race," which could be "accomplished by rezoning, pairing, grouping, and clustering elementary schools by rezoning and reordering the feeder system into the junior high schools and by the rezoning of the high schools." After examining the plan submitted by Mr. Mapp, he observed that extensive transportation of students, both to contiguous and noncontiguous school zones, would be required to effectuate Mr. Mapp's plan—in short, busing. But before considering Mr. Mapp's plan, however, Judge Wilson looked to the board's plan, feeling, as he had earlier said in enunciating the principal governing his review, that the board's plan should be adopted unless violative of equal protection. The board had proposed a unitary system for the elementary schools by closing five, pairing sixteen and clustering six, rezoning three, and leaving three unchanged. The board's plan, therefore, had only five exceptions to its own 30 percent to 70 percent requirement. Even though the board's plan did not necessarily meet the mathematical formula exactly, Judge Wilson found that "the board has carried the burden of establishing that the racial composition is not the result of any present or past discrimination on the part of the board or other state agency. Rather, such result is the consequence of demographic and other factors not within any reasonable responsibility of the board." Judge Wilson, therefore, approved the plan for elementary schools. No discrimination was found with respect to the middle schools, but with respect to high schools, however, he found the statistical data inadequate and inaccurate and declined to approve or disapprove the board's plan. He then requested that a new plan be submitted by the board in accordance with his opinion.

Judge Wilson correctly predicted a storm would follow his decision, and he then crafted an addendum to that opinion, which is a model of eloquence and will be reproduced in its entirety.

If understanding of the legal basis for the decisions heretofore made cannot be given, then the court can only appeal to the conscience of the community for that understanding. As anyone who has kept up with public affairs in recent times must know, Chattanooga is not being singled out for special judicial treatment. One has but to read to know that most of the major cities of this nation are contending with the problems here being judicially dealt with. The city of Chattanooga can never expect to remain an island within the nation living in the pre-*Brown v. Board of Education* era, when the rest of the nation is moving into the post-*Brown v. Board of Education* era. This city has made great progress in racial affairs in recent years. Though some were opposed at the time to that progress, few would not publicly propose that the racial clock be run back in Chattanooga to where it stood in 1960, and none would suggest that it be run back to where it existed a century ago.

This court is not insensitive to the fears and anguish expressed by some within the city in recent days, nor does it relish the abuse and worse that has been so abundantly shared by word and letter, but this court would be unworthy of trust in the least of its functions if it were to allow these things to cause it to deviate, in the least, from its sworn duty to uphold the Constitution and the laws as that Constitution and as those laws have been duly established and interpreted by the properly constituted authorities, including the United States Supreme Court and the Appellate Court under which this court functions. How can anyone expect this court to uphold the law of Congress regarding robbery of a bank but, in the face of public misunderstanding and criticism, turn its back upon the constitutional requirement that all citizens be treated equally before the law?

There may well exist basis for criticism of the interpretation placed upon the equal protection clause by the United States Supreme Court as it applies to public schools. But there can be not the least doubt that this court, as well as every court in the nation, is bound by that interpretation. Furthermore, who is so certain of the correctness of his own views of the equal protection clause that he would be willing to swap places in the social and racial scheme of affairs in our society? How many are so convinced of the correctness of their own interpretation of that clause that they would be willing to live in a society in which each man is free to make his own interpretations of all laws? Surely, thoughtful men must agree that the rule of law is the single greatest achievement of the centuries-long struggle for freedom.

This city can continue upon the path of orderly progress in racial harmony and all of its affairs, including the operation of its schools. This city can live within the law. This city can maintain and improve its program quality education for all children within his schools. This city can have one of the finest school systems within the state or within the nation, but it first must believe that it can. It must first want the finest schools for its children. Medieval Florence, a miserable hovel of a city compared with modern Chattanooga, gave America its name and the world the Renaissance. But it did it only because its leaders and as people believed that it could be done and will that it should be done.

And then he said this:

Equal protection of the law might not seem so heavy a burden for anyone to carry if he felt that it were truly his brother's child who was asking for it. Quality education might not seem so difficult for anyone to maintain if it were truly his brother's child that was being deprived or handicapped by its denial.

This city has seen its share of law violators, racial disharmony, fear, and distress in recent weeks and months. For those who believe that defiance of the law can be replaced with willing obedience, for those who believe that racial strife can be replaced with racial harmony, for those who believe that fear can be replaced with trust, for those who believe that quality education can be maintained and enlarged within the Chattanooga public schools, for those who believe that mankind can live in peace and harmony with his fellow man, for those who believe in the essential brotherhood of man, the bell tolls now.

The atmosphere in Chattanooga on segregation at that time was electric. For his decision, Judge Wilson received heaps of abuse, especially by the East Lake Advisory Council, which accused him of "gross negligence" in approving the board's plan. But the *Chattanooga Times* editorialized as follows: "Judge Wilson should not be the crucible for those who will not find the way to a conducive atmosphere."

Although he thought his opinion brought a conclusion to segregation in the City Schools, it reared its head again when a state court enjoined the use of funds by the City for busing. In response, Judge Wilson issued an order to showcase why the state court judgment should not be set aside. No one from the city spoke or appeared before him on that issue, and no appeal had been taken from the state court decision. Judge Wilson issued an injunction against the enforcement of the state court judgment, and he excoriated the refusal of the state courts to follow Supreme Court precedent:

Although these decisions are sometimes referred to by persons not knowledgeable in the law as "mere precedent," all persons with knowledge or respect for the law are fully aware that these unanimous decisions of the United States Supreme Court are the law of the land binding upon every person in the land and every court in the land, including the courts of Hamilton County, Tennessee, and this court. These matters are so clear as to render any contention to the contrary frivolous on its face.

Finally, he said that he had only acted to remove "all vestiges of racial discrimination...where such discrimination was shown to have been created by past or present actions of the state or local government. Nothing more nor nothing less than this has been ordered." For this ruling, the *Times* again editorialized that this order should "reaffirm all concerned citizens' faith in our judicial system."

In 1973, again refusing to relinquish the field, the Chattanooga Board of Education submitted a revised plan to the court after the 1971 decision had been affirmed by the Sixth Circuit Court of Appeals en banc with review denied by the Supreme Court. The board contended that a revision was necessary because of changed conditions—a declining enrollment because of white flight to the suburbs. The modification was denied because the legal issue was not the mixing of the races but equal protection, and that phenomenon "cannot become a higher value at the expense of rendering equal protection of the laws the lower value."

Judge Wilson's successor, Judge R. Allan Edgar, finally brought the case to an end. In doing so, Judge Edgar wrote, "Pursuant to the memorandum filed here with, plaintiffs' amended motion for further relief is hereby DENIED. The defendants' motion for relief from final judgment is likewise DENIED." Thus, Judge Edgar, too, probably continued Judge Wilson's irritation of both sides and left standing Judge Wilson's final decision, ending over twenty-six years of conflict over the desegregation of the Chattanooga City schools. The end of this legal marathon in 1986 ironically predated a political conclusion to the issue of segregation in the Chattanooga City schools. In the 1990s, the city of Chattanooga voted to go out of the business of public education and abdicated its education system to the county, whose school system had not been a party to the *Mapp* case. This political conclusion also ended three attempts to combine the city of Chattanooga and Hamilton County into a metropolitan form of government. The stumbling block in those three separate attempts, in which voters resoundingly rejected the merger of the two governments, was the fear of busing. County residents did not want their children having to travel downtown to go to school, and city residents did not want their children to have to go out into the county.

After a four-day hearing in October 1985, Judge Edgar, in concluding the case, found, "Without serious question the Court finds that the Board did in fact implement all aspects of the Plan which had received court approval—except in the area of desegregation of faculty and staff."

In closing the case, an irony was presented. In Judge Edgar's consideration of the case, the plaintiffs had argued that annexation by the city of Chattanooga had perpetuated segregation. When Judge Wilson had considered the case in its infancy in the early 1970s, he urged the city to accomplish desegregation even if it meant annexation. On that issue, Judge Edgar held, "There is no evidence in the record which would justify the conclusion that the racial makeup of the schools had anything to do with the decision of the city to annex adjacent areas. Thus, the court finds no intent to discriminate related to annexation." Nor did he find that discrimination was practiced in connection with school construction or school closings; a special committee appointed by the city superintendent of schools had recommended in the early 1980s the closing of twelve city schools for not being utilized.

Tennessee Valley Authority v. Allis-Chalmers

Until 1980, the Hoffa trial had been Judge Wilson's longest jury trial, consuming over eight thousand pages of transcript and two months of trial. But then came his longest civil jury trial. In fact, at the time, it was the longest civil jury trial in the history of the Federal Sixth Circuit (Michigan, Ohio, Kentucky, and Tennessee). That trial involved a Tennessee Valley Authority project just outside of Chattanooga. The project was a hydroelectric project on Raccoon Mountain called a pumped storage plant. A sophisticated utility such as the Tennessee Valley Authority can use a pump storage plant in its grid to use the excess energy created from its nuclear sources to pump water up to a reservoir in an elevated lake.

The operation of the pumped storage facility itself was fairly simple. The plant operated by the release of water from a reservoir above the Tennessee River on Raccoon Mountain. That water then flowed down to the Tennessee River through tubes called penstocks and into rings, called stay rings, which directed the water into the turbines to generate the electricity. The stay rings, which directed the water into the turbines, were made for TVA by Allis-Chalmers, and the steel was provided by Lukens Steel Corporation under a patent license from United States Steel Corporation. Being the largest pump storage plant in the world at that time was part of the problem. Normally, in other pump storage facilities, the stay rings were simply cast as a single piece. The Raccoon Mountain stay rings, however, were so large that they had to be fabricated from welded steel plates, and the welding required them to be "stress relieved" in a huge oven. After the stress-relieving process, however, the welds started to develop tiny cracks, and the stay rings had to be discarded, with the whole process starting over. TVA blamed its problem on Allis-Chalmers and the steel, asserting that the steel, known as T-1 steel, should not have been used by Allis-Chalmers to fabricate the stay rings. TVA and Allis-Chalmers settled their dispute, however, and joined forces and sued the steel companies, asserting that neither had been warned of the cracking that was encountered. TVA's claim was for $120 million worth of lost power due to the delay, and this was the setting for the trial.

This trial started on February 25, 1980, and lasted until August 20, 1980, each trial week being four days long.

Judge Wilson divided the case into three separate parts. In the first part, the jury was to determine whether the cases of the plaintiffs were barred by the statute of limitations by not having been brought in a timely fashion. If the jury decided in the first phase that the lawsuits were timely brought, the jury was then to determine whether Lukens and US Steel were liable to TVA and Allis-Chalmers. If liability of the steel companies was found to exist, the case would then proceed to the third phase—the determination of damages.

Jury selection resulted in a jury of twelve with four alternates in what was originally predicted to be a two-month trial. In May, the jury was given the case for decision on the first issue of whether the cases had been timely brought by TVA and Allis-Chalmers. On that issue, the jury found that they had been brought in a timely fashion and were not barred. The trial then continued on the issue of whether the steel companies were at fault by not warning of the propensity of the steel to crack when stress relieved. During that portion of the trial, expert after expert testified, prompting Judge Wilson to observe in his trial notes: "Where did these parties find these loquacious experts?" After all the evidence was submitted and closing arguments made, Judge Wilson submitted the case to the jury in a manner in which they could most easily understand, submitting the case to them twelve different times over almost a two-week period. When they reported their verdict, the jury found in favor of the steel companies, and the case ended without going to the third phase. Basically, the jury found that even if the steel companies had not given proper warnings, the plaintiffs had not been diligent in researching whether the use of the steel for the stay rings was appropriate.

Despite the seriousness of the case, there were some light moments, such as the time Judge Wilson received testimony of a witness out of the presence of the jury so that he could make a ruling as to whether the jury would be allowed to hear that witness. The witness was a metallurgical engineer employed by TVA. After an answer to one of the questions, TVA's lawyer, not liking the answer, commented, "Dr. Bressler, I don't think you understood my question," at which point Judge Wilson quipped, "Mr. Washburn, I don't think you understood his answer."

By the end of the trial, Judge Wilson had collected data for the benefit of counsel—actually, for the benefit of anyone. He found that TVA had used five lawyers during the trial, Allis-Chalmers had used seven, Lukens had used four, and US Steel had used nine, for a total of twenty-five lawyers. The trial had taken five months and twenty-five days, for a total of eighty-six trial days with eighty-nine witnesses, 16,825 pages of transcript, and 1,139 exhibits. He estimated the per day trial cost at $22,190 and the estimated cost of the whole trial at $1,974,000, and closing arguments of counsel consumed ten hours.

After recounting the data, Judge Wilson then made general comments for the guidance of the attorneys. His suggestions were always constructive, and the comments he made for this complex products liability-business trial could apply to any present-day trial of similar complexity.

Before he made his suggestions, however, he did something that he could not have done in the Hoffa trial: he complimented the attorneys, saying, "The attorneys for all parties were commendable for their courtroom decorum, courtesy, and professional representation of their clients." For the jury, he had nothing but praise, saying, "The trial demonstrates that even in a very protracted and very complex lawsuit, the jury is capable of making an intelligent verdict based upon the law and advice of the court."

In making other observations, he first criticized the defendants for not moving to dismiss the case at an early stage rather than waiting when there had been "37,500 pages of discovery and a genuine jury issue existed." A sidenote is worthy here. At a pretrial conference in chambers before the trial commenced, one lawyer was bold enough to ask when a ruling on the pending pretrial motions for summary judgment could be expected. Those motions sought to dismiss the case by asserting that there was no issue of fact for a jury to decide—that Judge Wilson should dismiss the cases on his own as a matter of law. Judge Wilson simply pointed to his conference table where those papers had been placed, standing over two feet high, and quipped, "The court can't help but think that somewhere in that stack of papers is a genuine issue of material fact."

In continuing his observations after the jury verdict, he also noted "some areas in which counsel could have improved presentation of the case":

(a) Discovery was greatly overdone by all counsel.

(b) The attorneys often overlooked the jury and proceeded with highly technical matters in a highly technical manner (i.e., one day we spent most of the day in cross-examining an expert on the calculus of crack propagation in metal.)

Another of Judge Wilson's pet peeves on which he commented in this trial was cross-examination. The cross-examination of Allis-Chalmers's chief engineer was "tedious and ineffective—areas of cross-exam should have been more carefully selected and then move quickly to the point." In other words, if you've got a point that the jury can understand, make it and sit down.

His positive comments included the following: "the attorneys should have prepared a chart with a glossary of terms used at trial," another chart "that reflected organization of each party and place in the organization of principal witnesses and otherwise identified witnesses at the start of trial. Since TVA and AC rely on a list of prior problems in the use of T-1, Lukens and US Steel should have prepared a list of users without any problems. The magnitude of the latter list would tend to overwhelm the first list." As to the damage allegedly suffered by TVA—delay and loss of cheap power—he felt "it was never clear to the court whether this type of damage would be recoverable under the various theories asserted," suggesting again the appropriate use of pretrial summary judgment motions and questioning the basis for TVA's case. The loss of the use of the pumped storage facility was TVA's main claim; it asserted that it could have used the hydroelectric power generated by the pump storage facility instead of the more costly gas turbine power.

Finally, there is one event that occurred during the trial that was absolutely startling to everyone, including Judge Wilson, and to recount it, no names have been used. During the deliberation of the jury during its latter stages, Judge Wilson's notes reflect a disclosure that was made at 11:15 one morning:

> Juror #42 _ Mr. X–Atty. Z played golf with him this weekend!
> (Reserve decision on nature and extent of sanction to impose
> on Z—i.e., reprimand or taxation of any additional costs.

One of the attorneys had actually played golf with one of the jurors during their deliberation process. Fortunately, no sanctions ended up being imposed because no harm was done.

After the Raccoon Mountain case had consumed his courtroom from February to August, Judge Wilson waited only about four weeks before launching into another jury trial that lasted the remainder of the year. But in between these two lengthy cases, he found time to consider the papers submitted to him in *Wiley v. Franklin*, a case that considered the constitutionality of the study of the Bible in the city and county schools. Thus, three cases consumed an entire year of trials for Judge Wilson.

In the Bible study case, the judge issued a landmark decision that many courts and school systems have used as a model for determining the constitutionality of biblical studies. The decision was the last of three decisions in the case that had originated a few years earlier. In it, he found the city's program constitutional but the county's unconstitutional. In his original decision, he struck down both programs as infringing upon the freedom of religion clause of the First Amendment but also held that a "legally permissible Bible study course would be academically and educationally desirable." The ultimate test, however, would depend upon "classroom performance." In making his 1980 determination, Judge Wilson listened to the tapes of the classes from the city schools and ten from the county schools. The guidelines that Judge Wilson used in assessing these classes were as follows:

> (1) Establish uniform minimum standards for the selection and employment of persons teaching Bible study courses in the elementary grades, which standards shall specifically exclude as a condition of selection for employment any religious test, any profession of faith or any prior or present religious affiliation; (2) establish a procedure for the release and replacement of all teachers currently teaching Bible study courses in the elementary grades who do not meet the minimum standards adopted pursuant to paragraph (1) above, such release and replacement to be accomplished within a period of 30 days after the Court shall have approved the minimum teacher standards; and (3) establish a plan whereby the school board or some duly designated school

staff member or other school personnel shall, without participation by any non-school person or organization, select and employ all Bible study course teachers and effect the placement, training and supervision of all such teachers.

After the school boards had adopted plans and hired personnel, an objection was immediately raised that a newly selected teacher had received education from a church-sponsored institution of higher learning. Judge Wilson quickly rejected that objection because such a barrier to a teacher would "be as impermissible as a religious test to require such a faith or religious educational background." In other words, a test that requires faith-based education as a requirement for teaching Bible is as bad as a test that prohibits it.

Judge Wilson, having listened to the tapes, found that the lessons taught in the city schools on the Bible neither advanced nor inhibited religion and that the city's program was constitutional. The tapes of three of the county's ten classes, however, showed that "the primary effect of the lessons would be to promote religious beliefs, and not to convey biblical literary, historical or social incidents, themes or information in a nonreligious or secular manner." The three classes had all discussed retribution resulting in the wrath of God for disobedience to Him.

The Hamilton National Bank Case (*Weems v. Yeomans*)

This case involved a traumatic event for the banking community in the city of Chattanooga—the closing of a bank by the Comptroller of the Currency and its takeover by the Federal Deposit Insurance Corporation. The bank, the Hamilton National Bank, was one of the only banks in the South to make it through the bank closings of the Depression in the 1930s, but it was closed on February 15, 1976, because of its precarious financial condition. The lawsuit resulting from its failure, whose trial started in 1980, was brought by the trustee in bankruptcy of the parent company, Hamilton Bancshares, and involved, as defendants, the officers and directors of Hamilton National Bank, its parent Hamilton Bancshares, and its directors and its accounting firm, Arthur Andersen. Ironically, the chief executive officer of the bank, in a cost-saving move, terminated the officer and director liability insurance coverage eleven months before the bank was closed without disclosing that fact to the officers and directors, thereby leaving them without insurance to defend themselves in the ensuing lawsuits.

After a lengthy two-and-a-half-month trial, the jury returned its verdict in favor of the defendants and the accounting firm. At the trial's conclusion, Judge Wilson made comments similar to those that he had made in August for the previous trial. Thus, he found that the plaintiff trustee had been represented by six attorneys, the individual defendants had been represented by five, and Arthur Andersen had been represented by six. The trial had taken forty-three trial days with 7,995 pages of transcript and 479 exhibits and involved complicated banking and accounting issues.

Reflecting on both trials, he commented generally that "the parties could have stipulated a great amount of the relevant matters and saved much time and expense both in the discovery stage and at the trial." Continuing, he said, "If only the attorneys at the start of the litigation would take the time and make the effort to state the undisputed matters and call upon their opponent to admit such matters, it would reduce the time and cost of litigation dramatically."

The year 1980 came to a tiring end for Judge Wilson, although in a very different way from the end of the Hoffa trial.

CHAPTER SIX

Those Other Decisions

Realization by man that he is slowly but certainly decaying not only the aesthetics of his environment, but the life sustaining capacity of that environment has caused a public outcry that sounds worldwide.

The above quote was not from a study of global warming in the year 2015 but from a decision penned by Judge Wilson in the 1970s. Frank Wilson was acutely aware not only of man's relationships with his fellow human being but also of man's relationship with his environment. This awareness may have started with what he saw in his World War II years in the devastation of the land and its inhabitants, but it was sharpened with his continued love and study of history, his appreciation of nature, and his witnessing of the civil and criminal conflicts in his courtroom.

Another observation with respect to Judge Wilson's decisions is appropriate at this point. Commentators feel compelled to devise statements about the legacy of a particular jurist, and some of these characterizations may be appropriate. Justice Oliver Wendell Holmes was famous for his advocacy of objective standards by which to judge the conduct of humankind, and that urging ultimately led to the creation of the "reasonable man" standard in judging whether certain conduct was legally permissible. The reasonable man was used as an objective standard to satisfy the requirements of the legal system. Judge Wilson, however, would more often use "societal expectations" in making that judgment to satisfy the requirements of the legal system. Some may say that the two standards are really the same, but they are not. What may be reasonable for one person in the context of the interaction of that one person with another person may not necessarily be what society or civilization demands of that person. Although Judge Wilson aspired to a higher societal standard, he was confined by legal precedent to the reasonable man.

Before discussing some of Judge Wilson's decisions other than *Hoffa*, *Mapp*, *TVA*, and *Weems*, the reader needs to understand how judicial decisions evolve. A federal judge has two judicial clerks who assist in the preparation of decisions. They are normally recent graduates of law school and assist by observing the trial and researching the legal issues involved with the judge's guidance. If the case is a nonjury case, they may prepare initial drafts of the decision after discussing Judge Wilson's initial beliefs as to the correct result. If the case involves a jury trial, they may assist in researching the law as to the evidentiary issues and the instructions to be given the jury.

The involvement of the clerks in the written decisions in a nonjury case is generally more involved than in a jury case. In that situation, the decision will contain a core that is often no more than a page or two of what may be a fifteen- or twenty-page decision, but that core is the soul of the decision. What has led up to that key portion is a recitation of the facts of the case and the legal precedent in the area of law involved. What follows the core is the explanation of how the result flows logically from the application of legal precedent to the facts of the case at hand.

In writing his decisions, Judge Wilson would first confer with his law clerks to discuss the case in general and to begin to discuss what legal principles should be applied. Was there established precedent settled by prior appellate decisions, often called stare decisis, or was he in what was known as new ground—an area of the law where the appellate courts had not yet spoken. If it were the latter, he would discuss with his clerks how far the law had progressed and whether they could predict where an appellate court might go in this new area.

He would then turn the opinion over to the law clerks for a first draft. After they finished their draft and returned it to Judge Wilson, they would not see it again until it was ready to be published. What Judge Wilson supplied in creating the final opinion was his artful language on what the conclusion would be—how the law should be applied to the facts to reach a conclusion that made sense and was justifiable. It was in this conclusion, the core, this justifiable end result, that Judge Wilson was most eloquent. And it was not just the words that he used that were eloquent; it was the justification imparted by these words that were eloquent. A common reaction to his decisions often was, "Well, how could it be any other way?"

The breadth of subjects on which Frank Wilson ruled was vast. A federal judge must deal with both civil and criminal cases, and on the civil side, they ranged from interpretation and enforcement of state and federal statutes to civil rights, labor disputes, environmental issues, and constitutional questions. But Judge Wilson always retained an uncommon sense of humor and an uncommon eloquence in reaching his decisions. An example of the humor with which he approached making a decision was his adoption of a prayer from a colleague in South Georgia, which describes very well the predicament of a federal judge in reaching decisions:

> Dear Lord, on bended knee, I pray you, tomorrow, send me a plain old tort case. Or if you can't do that, a suit on a simple contract in writing will do just as well. That's a little enough favor to ask even if I have gotten rusty on common law since I've been on this court.
>
> And deliver me, oh Lord, from any 2254s or 1981s, 1983s or, it can't be much worse than what we federal judges have under Title 42. And if you care about me, Lord, don't send me any class actions, whatever they are. It's not that I mind the work. You know me better than that, Lord. It's just that I'm not a pedagogist, tensorialist, restaurateur, literary

censor, or personnel director. And another thing, please don't put me on a three-judge court. Lord knows I got enough trouble agreeing with myself, much less trying to convince two other damn fools.

Now, Lord, I'm not going to try to run your business, but some day, you've got to put an end to the individual discrimination against me and give me the equal protection of the Ten Commandments and all recent amendments thereto.

Over his twenty-two years, Frank Wilson published over 250 opinions on a wide variety of subjects, many of which would be boring to the reader. But some of the more important and even humorous ones bear discussion. There was a diversity of subjects on which he wrote.

Before examining the more serious cases, however, any examination must start with a decision that was both serious and tongue-in-cheek. That case, early in his career, involved a student named Brownlee, who sued the Bradley County Board of Education. The case presented a constitutional issue not often considered in federal court—hair. No, this decision was not about the play *Hair* but rather the length of hair that might be grown by a Bradley County male student, who was expelled because his long hair was not in accord with the dress code adopted by the school in 1970. Judge Wilson described the issue he was to decide as follows: "The lawsuit involves the subject of human hair and its grooming upon the male of the species, a subject not thought of as grist for the judicial mills." After his tongue-in-cheek preamble, he found that the student preferred the hair length as a personal preference and not a statement of free speech. So by the student's own stated preference, Judge Wilson found that the First Amendment was not applicable. Since then, students have become wiser in stating their preference in constitutional terms. Judge Wilson went on to analogize the 1970 situation to a wild man from Borneo being dismissed as a court officer, finding that "the matter of decorum in the courtroom stands on no loftier rational nor constitutional basis than does decorum in the classroom." The policy was held valid, and the decision ended, as begun, with a quote, this from Pope, "O hads't though, cruel been content to seize Hairs less in sight or any hairs but these."

With that opening, there was another decision involving hair. This time, it was the off-Broadway rendition of *Hair*.

The producer of the play *Hair* sought to use one of Chattanooga's theaters for its production. The use was denied because nudity and obscenity were not going to occur in a Chattanooga theater at that time. A lawsuit then resulted from that denial. At trial, Judge Wilson impaneled an advisory jury to review the entire script of the play. An advisory jury is used occasionally by a judge as a sounding board. Its decision has no binding effect on the parties, but it may be reflective of the sense of the community on an important issue, such as obscenity and nudity. Since community values were to be involved in the issues in the case, Judge Wilson approached the case from a political, as well as legal, vantage point.

The advisory jury found that the production was obscene under a First Amendment standard because it was utterly without socially redeeming value. Because the jury was advisory only, Judge Wilson reviewed the script himself but without the obscene portions. When viewed in that fashion, he found he could not make the same finding that the jury had made. But when he judged the production under Tennessee's obscenity statute, however, he found that it was patently offensive and an affront to community standards and ruled that the theater could not be leased for the show. Finding that regulation of sex and undisciplined sexual conduct was within the police power of the state, Judge Wilson explained, "Undisciplined sex is one of the most destructive forces in any society and has historically been so recognized. It is destructive of many human values and institutions, not the least of which is the family, which in turn has served as the foundation for every civilization known to man." By deciding the case in this fashion, that is, under Tennessee's obscenity statute, he was able to avoid a direct conflict with the First Amendment's protection of free speech

After finding that *Hair* could not be produced, he took the federal government to task in a tax case. He refused to apply the intricate sections of the tax code as urged by the Internal Revenue Service and preferred instead to take on the government, mainly the Service, for not considering the law applied by the Federal Communications Commission. Taken together, he felt that the two agencies were taking inconsistent positions. In the case of WDEF Broadcasting, it was insisted it had a right to amortize the cost of construction of a broadcasting station and the value of its broadcast license over the life of the license, which was a limited period. The Internal Revenue Service said no and said the period should not be limited to the time period for which the license was valid but for an unlimited period of time. Judge Wilson found this position inconsistent with the position taken by another branch of the government—the Federal Communications Commission, which had granted the license but reserved the right not to renew it. Examining the big picture, Judge Wilson criticized the government for its inconsistency, stating, "It ill behooves the government to serve its regulatory ends by granting licenses of a definite, limited duration, reserving the power to grant or refuse renewal and, at the same time, to contend for tax purposes that the specified duration of such licenses should be disregarded." The decision was logical.

The Tennessee Valley Authority

As one might guess, there were Tennessee Valley Authority decisions, mainly involving TVA's acquisition of land for hydroelectric purposes. In 1966, Judge Wilson found that a landowner whose land was taken by TVA was not entitled to compensation because the value of the land with which he was left was greater than the whole parcel he started with because of improvements made by TVA to the land taken. So after TVA had taken part of the land, what the landowner was left with was worth more than the whole tract before it was taken—a result, again, that makes sense.

In another condemnation case a year later, a landowner tried to use the same argument by saying his land should be valued more because of TVA's improvements to land *near* the land taken, not on the land. Judge Wilson disagreed because it was not the owner's land taken that had caused the increase.

In a somewhat unusual 1975 business dispute, an unsuccessful bidder on a TVA contract argued that it should have gotten the contract because the successful bidder's specifications did not meet TVA standards. Judge Wilson disagreed, finding that the specifications were for the protection of TVA, not the disgruntled bidder.

When it came to blasting, Judge Wilson held TVA just as liable for property damage as any other blasted blaster.

Environmental

In a somewhat unusual decision in the area of environmental law in 1981, Judge Wilson sided initially with an environmental group, the Ocoee River Council, in a suit against TVA but then adopted a practical result. Initially, he agreed with the council and found that TVA had not considered the environmental impact of its power decisions but then gave TVA ninety days to do so. When TVA did take the environmental concerns into consideration in the ninety-day period, Judge Wilson dismissed the suit against TVA because it had justified the environmental concerns. But he had made them do what any good governmental agency should have done.

But TVA was not the only entity to present Judge Wilson with an environmental knot. Scholze Tannery, a Chattanooga plant, was a leftover from days when cow hides had to be tanned to be of use, and the by-product could be a bit odoriferous. An environmental group, the American Bass Anglers, took on the tannery, but not just the tannery; the federal government was also a defendant in what is known as a Qui Tam lawsuit where the environmental group assumed the role of the government and sued the tannery and the government for not doing its job to protect the environment—Chattanooga's pristine 1971 atmosphere. Remember, in 1969, Walter Cronkite had broadcast on the evening news that Chattanooga had the nation's dirtiest air.

Judge Wilson first said that the Anglers couldn't sue because they couldn't show special damage to them as a group. But Judge Wilson sensed the importance of the issue. Although he found that he could not order the Secretary of the Army or the Corps of Engineers to clean up the environment, he issued a timeless warning: "Technical proficiency and progress has had an unexpected and unwarranted by-product, ecological erosion. The extent of the erosion is not known at this point in time. But realization by man that he is slowly but certainly decaying not only the aesthetics of his environment but the life-sustaining capacity of that environment has caused a public outcry that sounds worldwide." So in one decision, he defended both the environment and judicial principles and also predicted a social concern that was to evolve into a giant.

His finding that the Bass Anglers did not have standing to sue because the plaintiff had not suffered any damage itself was echoed in another decision in a suit where he refused to enjoin the use of Cameron Hill in downtown Chattanooga as fill dirt for Interstate Highway 24 in Chattanooga.

Antitrust and Patents

In the arena of intellectual property and the antitrust laws, Judge Wilson was presented only occasional disputes. The first was in 1962 and was an unusual antitrust case. The plaintiff complained that the defendant had unlawfully refused to test the plaintiff's alarm, which resulted in a loss of sales for the plaintiff and an unlawful restraint of trade. Because the defendant was a testing company and not a producer of alarms and because the plaintiff could not show collusion between the testing company and other producers of alarms, the suit was dismissed.

In a 1963 decision, Judge Wilson dismissed a suit against Happy Valley Farms by Grant Patten Milk under the Clayton Act, which prevented anticompetitive mergers and acquisitions because the company acquired by Happy Valley was not a competitor of Grant Patten Milk.

In two other cases, plaintiffs complained of anticompetitive conduct, but Judge Wilson, by carefully looking at the big picture, said, "No foul." It might be anticompetitive conduct, but it was not done by a competitor.

His first patent infringement action came in 1970 where the defendant asserted the plaintiff's patent was invalid. The court found that the plaintiff's product patent was not valid because one skilled in the art could have practiced the invention, and it was not, therefore, unique. In a later patent infringement case, the result was the same. The design of a chicken feeder was found to be obvious to one skilled in the art, and the plaintiff's suit was dismissed. Now that decision may be argued to have been decided according to locality law. The design of a chicken feeder might be obvious to a boy from North Carolina and East Tennessee, but maybe not to a big-city boy.

Constitutional Issues

Surprisingly, very few of Judge Wilson's decisions were decided on constitutional grounds. In 1962, Judge Wilson held that common law slander was not within the ambit of civil rights protection under federal law. In 1973, an inmate died and sued Hamilton County, alleging he had been assigned to a hazardous task; Judge Wilson found that the assignment might have been negligence and subject the county to suit in state court, but it was not a violation of a constitutional right, which would have allowed him to sue in federal court. The same result was obtained on similar allegations the next year in another inmate case. It must be remembered that these two plaintiffs had strained to get their controversies heard in federal court, but they failed. Although they may have pursued state remedies, the politics of the state courts was different, as might be remembered from the state court injunction against using city funds for busing in the *Mapp* case.

In 1981, Judge Wilson was quick to see through subterfuge by the state of Tennessee where the state created a court of limited jurisdiction to try a lesser included offense, leaving it to another court to try the main offense. This was an obvious case of the state trying to get two bites at the apple, and Judge Wilson found that it was a nice try but still double jeopardy—the prohibition of which the state could not avoid by creating a court of limited jurisdiction where the lesser included offense could be tried.

Whiskey and Drugs

Early in his career on the bench in 1962, Judge Wilson had a number of cases involving whiskey violations. Today, these cases would have focused on drugs, not whiskey. But the drug offenders have become smarter than the moonshiners. In one case, a motion to suppress evidence of the sale of illicit whiskey that had been obtained by binocular observation of the defendant's house was denied, and the evidence was allowed to be used because there was no trespass. This was an obvious case where the curtains should have been closed.

When drugs began to be more portable, such as heroin, "bystanders" started to suffer. When a Cadillac was forfeited in its transportation of heroin, the bank complained of the confiscation of their security for a loan to acquire the Cadillac. But Judge Wilson decided that the rights of the bank were no better than those of the owner. If the case had been a moonshine case instead of a drug case, Bobby Allison would've outrun the revenooers, and the car would never have been lost.

In another whiskey case, a warrant may have been defective, but the evidence was not suppressed because the crime was committed in the presence of the officer—the moral: don't drink your own product in front of the cops.

In 1964, a prisoner's sixth motion to set aside his conviction was considered and denied, Judge Wilson observing, "It is apparent that the petitioner has diligently followed appellate decisions in the field of criminal law during his period of confinement." This is what happens when prisons afford inmates law libraries.

In another rather unique criminal case, the defendant asked for new trial because of an outburst by the victim from the witness stand. Judge Wilson was canny enough to see that the defendant might make the request for a new trial, so in addition to instructing the jury to disregard the outburst, he went further, and when the jury returned its verdict, he asked each juror whether the outburst affected the verdict. Each juror said that they had followed Judge Wilson's instruction and had not considered the outburst. A new trial was avoided by quick thinking.

Corporations and Their Existence

Judge Wilson also had to deal with what courts have grappled with for a long time and with more publicity recently—what is a corporation, and does it exist as a person? The Supreme Court of the United States recently discussed this issue in connection with political contributions, but Judge Wilson was presented with the question, Where does a corporation exist? Well, he said, if it mines coal here and makes money here, it is in Tennessee.

Issues sometimes arose about where a defendant corporation could be sued and, more particularly, whether it could be sued in Tennessee. The most obvious choices are the state in which it was formed, the state in which it does business, and the state where it has "significant contacts." This latter choice often creates the most confusion. In a case involving the Hamilton National Bank, Judge Wilson said that a borrower who delivered a note in Tennessee and pledged stock for it could be sued in Tennessee on the note where the proceeds were delivered in Tennessee. But if a defendant had only pledged stock in Tennessee as collateral for the note, he could not be. Just six months later, Judge Wilson held, however, that a company from outside the state could not be sued where the contacts of the company were minimal, even though the corporation was licensed to manufacture articles in Tennessee and its representatives had visited Tennessee to inspect the plant and explain the manufacturing process. That case was one of the few times Judge Wilson was reversed, and the decision became one of the leading decisions in the Sixth Circuit (Michigan, Ohio, Kentucky, and Tennessee) over the ability of foreign corporations to be sued away from their home state.

Labor Law

In the area of labor law, there were, as might be expected, more frequent decisions. The first, in 1963, received a great deal of notoriety. The trial was attended by a number of national labor leaders. In the case, the plaintiff, Paul Gibbs, had been hired by Grundy Company, a subsidiary of Tennessee Consolidated Coal Company, as a mine superintendent to open a new mine and then as a contract hauler of coal. Tennessee Consolidated had laid off one hundred UMW miners when it had previously closed a mine, and Gibbs was going to use miners from the UMW's competitor, Southern Labor Union. The UMW workers, however, believed they had been promised these jobs and, arming themselves, prevented the opening of the mine. After the international union stepped in and established a picket line, no further violence occurred, but Gibbs lost his jobs. He sued the international union, not the local, for a secondary boycott under the Taft-Hartley Act and under state law for contract interference. The jury found that there was a violation of the secondary boycott provisions of the Taft-Hartley Act and of common law because the violent picketing on his first day of work prevented him from working. Judge Wilson had said the plaintiff could sue on both theories. Although Judge Wilson found that there was no violation of Taft-Hartley, he sustained the jury finding of violation of state law. He was affirmed by the Sixth Circuit, but the case went to the Supreme Court, which resulted in a reversal. The Supreme Court held that for the International Union to be liable, it would have had to have been involved in the violence, but the evidence failed to show that. Gibbs was limited to recovery under Taft-Hartley.

Allegedly, illegal picketing was again before the court on an application for a temporary restraining order to prohibit picketing, which had shut down all Grundy County coal mines. Judge Wilson found a violation of the statute existed and issued the restraining order, in part to permit the orderly handling of a petition for certification of the union. Less than a month later, the case was back before the court with the union and the NLRB seeking to set aside the injunction. The employer sought to intervene to oppose the set-aside, but Judge Wilson denied the request to intervene, stating that the court could not permit a private party to control the activity of the NLRB and that an injunction could not be continued if the applicant did not want it continued. Although intervention was denied, Judge Wilson did state that he might "desire to avail [himself] of helpful suggestions."

In another "hair" case, Judge Wilson refused to compel arbitration, where an employee discharged for failure to shave was joined by fellow employees who engaged in an unauthorized walkout and who themselves were then discharged. Judge Wilson refused to compel arbitration because the contract did not require it, quoting in his opinion a statement by a union representative who said, "Such is the human nature of labor-management controversies that small and foolish things [beards] can sometimes spark a major controversy."

Tax Cases

Although tax cases might be unusual to the layperson, they are not to a federal judge, and Judge Wilson decided at least six of them. In one of the first, Judge Wilson refused to allow avoidance of tax in a foreclosure where it was a foreclosure between related corporations, finding that the value in the hands of the transferee was the same as in the hands of the transferor. Otherwise, related corporations would simply transfer their assets to avoid taxes.

Then in another case, Judge Wilson adopted the "common sense" approach of the taxpayer over the "rather involved process" proposed by the government. It seems that the government was trying to argue that a loss from an ice storm was not a casualty loss. Judge Wilson basically decided that the government was the casualty.

In a suit for estate taxes, Judge Wilson found that heirship by a son whose father was unmarried and aged fifty-four was not only practically impossible but also medically impossible. So much for octogenarians and Abraham.

In another momentous tax decision, he decided that payments to a civil service retiree were the result of disability and not subject to income tax. The amount of the disability payment was $363.35. Thus, there is no claim too small for federal court.

But then came a doctor's pension plan where he agreed with the IRS that the plan discriminated in favor of prohibited participants, and any attempt to amend the plan came too late.

Bankruptcy Cases

Despite the fact that appeals from bankruptcy court are taken to federal district court, there were surprisingly few bankruptcy decisions, and those were generally in later years after Judge Wilson's contemporary, Judge Ralph Kelley, retired. Judge Kelly rendered decisions that were generally unassailable or because Judge Kelly was able to work out so many compromises. In one of the first, however, a bankrupt had been denied a discharge of his debts because he had submitted false affidavits. His defense was "Everybody in the industry does it." The bankrupt lost; the judicial system trumps industry practice.

There is one procedural case worth mentioning. In a shipping case, Judge Wilson adopted a somewhat unusual procedure in deciding the case. He gave his opinion but stated that it would be based "on facts to be stipulated within 10 days of the opinion." Otherwise, he said he would take proof to establish them. You read that right. He decided the case based upon facts to be stipulated *after* the decision.

This discussion of Judge Wilson's cases will end with a series of cases that presented unusual stand-alone situations. In the first, Judge Wilson deferred to the jurisdiction of the Interstate Commerce Commission on the issue of the reasonableness of the rail service provided—let the regulator decide.

In another, he dismissed an action by students who alleged that part of their fees went to activities that they did not support. Popularity of an issue, he said, is not an issue for the court; the issue is reasonableness, and here the fees were rationally related to the operation of the university. You guessed it, University of Tennessee.

In a power board case, Judge Wilson found that a gross charge of 10 percent on an electrical bill was not usurious because it was not payment for the use of money or forbearance from collection.

And then an employer who terminated an employee for not reporting to work on his Sabbath was found not to be in violation of the religion clause because the employer could not give accommodation without unduly harsh results.

CHAPTER SEVEN

His Speeches

No tyranny could long exist that leaves a citizen's freedom
in the hands of twelve of his countrymen. So, a jury trial is
more than an instrument of justice. It is a lamp that shows
that freedom lives.

—Speech to the Judicial
Conference of the Sixth Circuit Court of Appeals

Both before and after he assumed the bench, the demand for Frank
Wilson to speak spanned the South. Although the subjects were
diverse, they generally fell into the categories of crime and its causes
and solutions, criminal rehabilitation, the Constitution of the United
States, the morality of mankind, history and education, and the impact
of greed upon society.

In his political career, before his confirmation as a federal judge,
Judge Wilson gave three speeches that demand our attention—other
than the speeches he made running for Congress. In August 1948, he
was interviewed on WROL, Knoxville, speaking as the second district
congressional campaign manager for Estes Kefauver's run for the United
States Senate. Because of the impact of that speech, he was asked to

repeat it the next night. In part of the speech, he spoke of the politicians of 1948 as follows, differentiating Estes Kefauver from them:

> And now I would like to say a few things about what I've learned since undertaking this campaign. In the first place, I've learned why many professional politicians so richly deserve the public contempt with which they are viewed— how they operate purely from motives of personal power and plunder rather than being motivated by principles; how they give their word, only to break it; how they flout every principle of fairness and decency to win elections. Learning this, I've learned why Mr. Kefauver selected his managers and workers from the ranks of the political "greenhorns"—if you please, citizens whose only desire and whose only reward will be the satisfaction of restoring government to the people and electing a statesman to the Senate.

Those words, uttered in 1948, seem to ring true today—perhaps even more so.

Later that month, speaking to Oak Ridge Jaycees, he suggested what they could do for their country. He gave them hope that all of them, not a privileged few, could make America a better place in which to live:

> To have an opportunity to participate in solving these problems is what it means to me to be an American. Every country in the world has its problems, many with much greater problems than ours, but America is one of the few remaining countries in which the average John Doe has an opportunity to participate in solving these problems.

As he continued in that speech, we see that his observations during World War II did have an impact on him, for he continued as follows:

> When I am tempted to withdraw from community activity and "Let George do it," I remember the story of Tony, a sixteen-year-old Italian boy who lost all his relatives in the

recent war. We had picked him up down in Sicily, and he
had followed our unit all through the Italian campaign.
As we were preparing to leave Italy, he came to me and
expressed the hopelessness that must be the lot of the
younger generation in many European countries today. He
explained that he was at a loss to know what to do when
the Americans left and ended up by saying that "mine is a
generation without happiness in the present or hope in the
future." It's up to every good Jaycee to make certain that no
American boy will ever feel the inclination to make such a
statement.

Then in February 1957, he made a memorable speech to the East
Tennessee Bar Association on one of his favorite topics, the Constitution
of the United States, and suggested that it was created to be a vibrant
document of self-governance to be used as a check, both on the excesses
of the government and on the relationship of its citizens, one to another.

Perhaps the first proposition that should be remembered
in construing and interpreting the Constitution is the fact
that it is not to be construed in the same manner that one
would interpret a statute or a contract for the reason that
the Constitution (including all amendments) makes general
provisions to meet conditions of the present and the future.
The framers of the original Constitution obviously had in
mind that there would be much development in the new
republic—did not know what it would be but made general
arrangements of principles to meet conditions as they came
along.

The rights and liberties of the people were protected against
encroachments by governmental power, and in fact, the
provisions of the Magna Carta were incorporated into the
Bill of Rights. Plainly, these provisions were limitations upon
all the powers of government, legislative as well as executive
and judicial.

> Another rule of interpretation is that the Constitution is not limited to the specific purpose for which it was adopted. That is to say, the Constitution was not intended to be a specific document that will encompass any situation that might develop and be covered by the provisions. While the powers granted to the general government do not change, they apply from generation to generation to all things to which they are, in their nature, applicable.

Clearly, what Frank Wilson related was an understanding, not just of the words of the document but also of the intent, meaning, and spirit of the document, as seen in the context of what the framers had accomplished and intended to accomplish in forming a government and the protection of the rights of its citizens.

Shortly after his confirmation as federal judge, he began his civic speeches, which were almost as significant and reflective of his wisdom as his decisions. During the time period from 1962 until his death in 1982, not only was Judge Wilson deciding momentous cases and authoring significant decisions, but his oratory was also ringing in the community. In over fifty speeches delivered over eighteen years, he mixed humor with pith, and his audiences ranged from an installation address for a First Christian minister in Athens, Georgia, to Rotary clubs across the state of Tennessee, to the University of Tennessee (Knoxville and Chattanooga), and the League of Women Voters, to name just a few.

Many of the speeches started with self-deprecation, followed by a story about one of his heroes, Winston Churchill. It seems that Sir Winston, returning from a banquet, was queried about whether he had enjoyed it, and he responded, "If the wine had been as old as the chicken and the chicken as young as the maiden and the maiden as willing as the duchess, it would have been a great success."

One theme that appeared early and continued throughout his speeches was the undue emphasis our society places on material things. For example, at the Chattanooga Brotherhood Week dinner on February 20, 1962, he said,

The problem we face is that with all the progress which the world is making in so many directions—in science and letters and fine arts and every form of industry, commerce, and transportation—why is it that there still exists so much misery, so many warped lives, so much want, and so much hardship?

If those who believe in the God of Moses and the brotherhood of mankind under one God cannot or will not provide the answer, then the priests and apostles of materialism will rush in to fill the void—and that is exactly what we have seen in our generation. With the vast increase in world population, more people experience and suffer from hunger, nakedness, squalor, and disease this very night and have so suffered in all of the previous history of mankind combined.

The issue in the world today is as to which culture (whether the Judeo-Christian culture tracing its origin back to Moses that founds a brotherhood of man upon a belief in one God) can continue to exist in the world and be the way to the future or whether the philosophy of materialism shall ruin the destinies of man.

This theme continued in an undated speech in which he described the marks of a religious man. In describing that person, whose faith was not in any particular religion, he was talking about a "moral" person, a person whose "real religion isn't just what he says it is or thinks it is but is what he does seven days a week." And returning to his theme of greed, he said of this religious man: "The material success attained by the men of today is indeed great, but this success has been and is bought by an indifference to the most elementary demands of morality, and there are more people in poverty and suffering than ever before."

In the *Oak Ridger* of March 26, 1962, Judge Wilson wrote on that same subject of brotherhood and compassion but stepped back, as he often did, and looked at the "big picture" of things. Thus, putting it all in context, he looked at mankind beyond the comforts of our neighborhood, when he broadly observed,

What a tragedy it would be if those whose only program is one of anger, intemperate charges, and suspicion of their fellow Americans were to come to positions of leadership. To those who may think that racial or religious intolerance, prejudice, self-sufficiency, sword-rattling, and anger are a sufficient answer to the problems America faces in the world today, I would just like to cite just a few facts:

- most of the people in the world live in Asia
- most of the world is nonwhite
- most of the world is abysmally, abjectly poor
- most of the world is wholly undeveloped
- most of the world is ill fed, ill housed, ill clothed to, illiterate
- most of the world is non-Jewish and non-Christian
- most of the world is non-English speaking
- most of the world is in revolution or has recently attained independence
- most of the world differs from us.

"Differs from us"—and yet we prosper and worry about our next vacation.

In 1965, he spoke to the annual meeting of the Tennessee Bar Association and started a serious speech with his normal humorous introduction. He told of the judge who had taken ill and received well-wishes from the local bar association, which had wired the judge: "We wish to extend our best wishes for your prompt and full recovery—by vote of 18 to 17." But then he turned to his serious subject—the history of the Sixth Amendment right to counsel. Although he started with *Gideon v. Wainwright,* he pointed out that the right to appointed counsel actually arose in a local case, the Scottsboro boys' case of *Powell v. Alabama,* in which the Supreme Court intervened in a state proceeding through the use of the due process clause of the Fourteenth Amendment. He noted that, originally, the right to counsel resulted through the interaction between state and federal courts and the Sixth and Fourteenth Amendments but had been reserved for capital cases. Because of the recent extension of the law by the Supreme Court at that time, he did something that he rarely did and criticized the Court for an extension of the law without completely balancing the competing interests. Thus, he said, "The fairness of a system of criminal justice cannot be measured solely in terms of avoiding the conviction of the innocent, though that is properly its first purpose. The conviction of the guilty is also a matter of concern. Otherwise, the millennium of criminal justice will have arrived when our trial processes shall have made it impossible to convict anyone." Interestingly, he omitted from his discussion another famous turn-of-the-century case from Hamilton County, Tennessee, of which, in fairness, he may not have known because of its recent notoriety. In that case, the Supreme Court had intervened for the first time in a state criminal proceeding by granting a writ of certiorari on the issue, not of the right to counsel but on the issue of the fairness of a state trial proceeding. The case involved the last person lynched from the Walnut Street Bridge in Chattanooga, Tennessee, Ed Johnson, and was the only criminal case actually tried in the Supreme Court. In it, the court held the sheriff of Hamilton County in contempt for allowing the lynching of the man whose safekeeping it had given to the sheriff of Hamilton County. The decision of the Supreme Court to intervene in a purely state court matter was the subject of bitter complaint in Chattanooga. The irony is that the Scottsboro boys and Ed Johnson are buried in the same cemetery in Chattanooga.

A few months later, in August 1965, after the extensive and intensive media coverage of the Hoffa trial, Judge Wilson spoke to a teachers' workshop at the University of Chattanooga on the subject of a free press and a fair trial, eloquently urging, "I cannot see why this nation be called upon to sacrifice the First Amendment on the altar of the Sixth, not the reverse thereof. The ultimate responsibility for a free trial rests upon the judiciary." He went on, however, to balance these two interests further when he said, "I know of no greater bulwark to the preservation of fair trials than the continuation of a free press, but freedom of the press is the right of the public to know, not merely the right of any particular publisher to report as he chooses." The speech was reported and repeated in many national publications and reflects, even more today, an almost perfect balance between the two constitutional protections.

In October 1966, Judge Wilson was appointed by Chief Justice Earl Warren to a twelve-judge committee to study proposed changes in the operation of juries in the federal system under the civil rights law. Before this time, federal juries were selected from state jury pools, but it was felt that those jury pools were not truly representative. A change earlier in 1960 had used the state lists but also used tax rolls and voter registration lists. On March 26, 1968, Judge Wilson was invited by special telegram to attend the signing of the resulting Federal Jury Reform Bill at the White House, greeted by President Johnson, and given a signing pen.

Then three months later in May, Judge Wilson spoke at the National Cemetery and urged, "Let us hear anew our promise to preserve that spirit of tolerance, that spirit of goodwill, the spirit of brotherhood that allows each individual to take his own thoughts, speak his own mind, worship according to the dictates of his own heart."

In February 1968, again addressing a meeting of the Tennessee Bar Association, Judge Wilson spoke on the Constitution and the Supreme Court. Observing that recent decisions of the court have disturbed many, this time, he defended what many perceived as unwarranted extensions of the law by the court when he said, "Personal philosophy of individual judges, rather than judicial tradition and legal precedent, has played an increasing role in decisions," but he said he was not there to criticize but rather to "stop and reflect upon the polestars, lest in our zeal to criticize or correct we do not cast aside fundamental values along with more immediate values of our criticism." He then discussed three eras of the court's decisions and ended by observing,

> Those who, by reason of displeasure or disagreement with any opinion or opinions of the court, would alter or destroy the great principles of judicial review, separation of powers, judicial independence, and judicial supremacy in the field of constitutional interpretation would not only destroy the works of John Marshall but, with them, would destroy constitutional government as we have known it for 179 years.

The United States of America would no longer be the United
States of America.

The speech echoed in many ways a speech he gave to the
Chattanooga Rotary Club on law enforcement in August 1967, when
he said that "the decay of a free nation begins when its citizens seek to
turn responsible freedom into in irresponsible indulgences, liberty into
license, respect for law into disobedience, and indignant concern into
apathetic indifference." He obviously experienced some of these issues
when he decided *Mapp*.

Later that year, he spoke on what was perhaps his favorite subject, the
jury system, the preservation of which he emphasized in his sentencing
of Jimmy Hoffa. He spoke to the Judicial Conference of the Sixth
Circuit Court of Appeals in May, and for his love of that system, he said,

> The jury system was never designed to work. Rather, it
> worked, and then men began designing it. Blackstone did
> as much to influence the nation's attitude toward the jury
> system when he said, "For the most powerful individuals
> in the state will be cautious of committing any flagrant
> invasion of another's right, when he knows that the fact of
> his oppression must be examined and decided by twelve
> indifferent men, not appointed until the hour of trial, and
> that, once when the fact is ascertained, the law must of
> course redress it. This, therefore, preserves in the hands
> of the people that share which they ought to have in the
> administration of public justice."

Judge Wilson then summed up by saying,

> When freedom is threatened in the world and when the
> power and influence of government becomes so all-pervasive
> and all-encompassing in our daily lives, we must look for
> some landmark of which we can say, "So long as it stands
> we are safe, and if it is threatened, we must resist." I suggest
> that no surer landmark could be found than the Anglo-
> American jury. For the jury is the essence of democracy. The

preservation of the jury is of the essence to the preservation of democracy. I cannot see one dying and the other surviving. No tyranny could long exist that leaves a citizen's freedom in the hands of twelve of his countrymen. So jury trial is more than an instrument of justice. It is a lamp that shows that freedom lives.

This speech, though, was overshadowed five years later, on April 11, 1973, when he gave a history of the Supreme Court at the University of Tennessee. That speech was so significant and noteworthy of study by law students that it was attached as part of this book as an appendix. He started that discussion of the Court by starting with the Constitution: "There has been much criticism of the Supreme Court decisions in recent years—most of it unworthy of serious discussion. We must start, however, with the Constitution itself proven to be the most enduring fundamental charter of government ever devised by man. On some points, there was agreement and on others compromise. But on the weightier problems that might well have prevented ratification, had specifics been stated, the framers of the Constitution either remained silent or used broad and indefinite language, thereby leaving such problems largely for posterity to settle."

In continuing his description of the Constitution, Judge Wilson observed that the document was both a compromise and a dodge. The compromise often occurred on issues that divided Northern and Southern states, such as taxation and the importance of a strong federal government. Other issues were dodged, and those were issues that were incapable of compromise, such as slavery. As Judge Wilson observed,

The Constitution clearly established a few principles about which there was no serious colonial disagreement...But still weightier difficulties that may have prevented ratification were either left severely alone by the founding fathers or treated in ambiguous clauses that passed the problem to posterity.

And that passage to posterity has often led to present-day disagreement between factions as to the manner in which the Constitution should be interpreted and even the possible legislative encroachment upon the powers of the judiciary because of legislative disagreement with the judiciary on political issues covered by the Constitution.

His speech then turned to a discussion of the Supreme Court and a history of their decisions, and he pointed out that there have been "three broad historical periods of Constitutional interpretation. Those periods were from 1789 to the close of the Civil War; 1865 to the 1937, the court revolution; and 1937 to the present." In the first period, he noted that the dominant theme was the value of the preservation of the American Union, while in the second period, the Court molded policy toward business and the protection of the business community against government intervention. The third period focused on the due process clause and was the civil rights era.

In discussing the first period, he gave historical context to such cases as *Marbury v. Madison* by discussing the intense conflict between the Federalists under President John Adams and the Republicans under President Thomas Jefferson. The climax of the conflict between those political factions occurred at the end of the first period with the *Dred Scott* decision, which created the climax in the alienation of both Southern and Northern contingencies on slavery and led to the election of an "obscure ex-Congressman President of the United States." This, of course, was Abraham Lincoln.

After discussing the second and third eras generally, he ended this memorable speech by noting that there has been severe criticism of the current Supreme Court decisions and concluded, "I sometimes find myself among the critics. I sometimes feel that I have cause to believe that individual members of the court have acted less judicial and more as an oracle or social architect than becomes any judge in a common law system." *But*…and here Judge Wilson issued an appropriate warning,

> Finally, when I criticize, I am reminded, and I would remind
> others, that while fair-minded and constructive criticism is
> a good thing for any institution in a democracy, including

the judiciary at all levels, it is equally true that ill-informed and intemperate criticism of the courts only serves to breed misunderstanding and incite disobedience to the law.

The rule of law is the greatest achievement of the centuries-long struggle for freedom. The acceptance of the rule of law, even that law with which one may personally disagree, and the use only of orderly procedures to change that law is the mark of a civilized person and is the mark of a civilized nation.

As earlier noted, two favorite subjects of his speeches were education and history, on the importance of which in a civilized society he spoke at a Rotary district conference. In that timeless speech, he said, prompted by reading a paper by a well-respected educator, that "one-half of the adult population of the United States was 'functionally illiterate.'" He then cited other statistics by which he was disturbed because they exist "in the paradox of living an era when it was never easier to be educated, but it was never harder to be intelligent." Continuing with that theme, he pointed out that we are in an era "in which it was never easier to accumulate knowledge than now but never more difficult to acquire wisdom."

In worrying about the lack of historical understanding, he gave an example of students who visited his courtroom during a trial but who said that they did not understand the portion of his jury charge that told the jury that they should not disfavor a defendant for his failure to testify. This question, he reflected, showed a lack of understanding of the historical perspective of our Constitution and to the "extent that the right is not understood and appreciated against its historical background, it stands in danger of being lost. So it is with freedom of the press, freedom of speech, and the other great freedoms that go to make up our democratic way of life. Without an understanding of the historical origin of the many freedoms we enjoy, those freedoms are in genuine danger of being lost." Has society progressed even further down this trail about which Judge Wilson warned fifty years ago? Have we become a society, where, as he said, "[p]eople without a sense of history, when forced to choose, love things more than ideas, love material society more than liberty, and always are in danger of losing both"?

About a dozen years after he delivered his warning about the lack of attention to history, he gave a follow-up to the men's club of Signal Crest United Methodist Church and started with one of the end points of the prior speech by pointing out it was error "to produce men with intelligence but without morals, to produce men with ability but without scruples, or to produce men with courage but without honor." He then described an unknown but great gentleman of Kentucky, of whom he learned after trying a case in Frankfort. On the way home, he stopped at the home of Henry Clay to learn a little history on the way home. There, he learned of the abolitionist Cassius Marcellus Clay. Although he was no kin to the boxer who used his hands as fighting tools, this Clay used his hands deftly with his bowie knife and was Lincoln's ambassador to Russia after having not been selected as his running mate. So Judge Wilson followed his own advice and learned history on the road from Frankfort to Chattanooga.

In a 1971 speech to the Chattanooga Chamber of Commerce Judge Wilson aptly played a version of role reversal with the Chattanooga business community by discussing what businessmen could/should expect from the law and what the law could/should expect of businessmen. In discussing business expectations of the law, he adverted to some of the principles of the decisions in the second period of Supreme Court decisions by stating what was to be expected was stability by providing predictability. Then he turned the tables and discussed what the law expected of businessmen. He listed three categories of businessmen— those who do what they can get away with, those who do only what they have to, and those who "do what a disciplined conscience tells any good man to do." He closed by saying,

> It is a matter of historical fact that one of the reasons why we have big government today is because some businessmen never learn the first lesson of free enterprise, namely, that freedom stays only where self-discipline prevails. Every sharp practice, every dishonest act, every false or misleading

misrepresentation, every compromise with principle weakens
the free enterprise system and weakens democracy itself.

We now come to two subjects about which Judge Wilson spoke but
also one for that he truly gave of himself: rising crime and the plight of
the prisoner. Prisoners, he said, came from that portion he referred to
as the untouchables—those who lived for crime and whom the church
and other saving institutions had not touched.

At the time he gave a particular speech in 1965, the cost of crime
in the United States was $27,000,000,000. He raised the issue of the
question of fault—Whose fault was crime? he queried. Was it education,
poverty, racial tension, breakdown of family? He continued with
that question in a number of speeches until he gave a talk in 1969
to the Rotary District Conference in Cleveland, Tennessee, where he
attempted to give three answers to his questions. His suggested solutions
were the following: (1) support of local law enforcement with proper
pay, (2) rehabilitation, and (3) conveying meaning, objectives, and
convictions to the youth with better education about meanings in life.
This latter solution he proposed through support of groups such as the
YMCA, Scouts, Boys Clubs, and the like. For his second solution, he
then gave an example of prisoners he had recently visited: ten inmates in
Ashland, Chillicothe, and Terre Haute. These were only 10 among the
150 he sentenced annually. From these, he received about one thousand
letters per year. Although only a fraction of those who had written him
showed any hope for change, Judge Wilson reached out to those to help,
and he urged others to do so too. To solve the problem, he said, "It is
not enough to preach in fine churches to the comfortable, the well-
to-do, the satisfied, the righteous, and the self-righteous." He urged his
audience to go to the source for help—to the prisoner.

CHAPTER EIGHT

The Wit and the Private Man

To be able to describe the private side of Frank Wilson would be difficult, but with the help of Frank Hill, probably his best friend, some insight can be gained. He and Frank Hill taught an adult Sunday school class at Signal Crest United Methodist Church, and the two mixed faith-based teaching with the history related in the Bible. For example, in one class, in order to discuss the development of the Hebrew peoples, it was necessary to discuss the "last great world power of the Bible to come on the stage." To do that, they "thought it might be in order to briefly mention the five other great world powers...which significantly influenced the development of the Hebrew peoples." They traced that history from the "fabled city of Ur" to the Fertile Crescent to Egypt, back to the Promised Land, through Assyria to Babylon, to the Persians and the Medes, to Greece, and finally to the Roman giant, "which was present for the greater portion of the development of the Christian era." It may have been Judge Wilson's attention to the importance of the historical teachings of the Bible, along with his love of history, that played a role in upholding the teaching of Bible in the Chattanooga City schools as the teaching of history, not the practice of a particular faith.

Not only did Frank Wilson and Frank Hill share a love of history, they also shared their children—Frank Wilson's sons, Frank and Randy, and Frank Hill's sons, Russell and Mark. Not only did they watch them grow and compete, they also saw Randy become a member of the Baylor School football team, which, in 1972, was ranked number 1 nationally.

Their friendship was so strong that in 1974, Frank Wilson, referring to a quote from Justice Oliver Wendell Holmes, wrote a tribute to Frank Hill: "To my friend Frank Hill, who runs the tightest ship and has the finest sense of direction of anyone I know." The quote from Holmes to which he referred reads as follows:

> I find the great thing in this world is not so much where we stand as in what direction we are moving...We must sail sometimes with the wind and sometimes against it—but we must sail and not drift, nor lie at anchor.

Not only did Frank Wilson love history, he also loved the great outdoors, and where better to enjoy them than the mountains of Tennessee and North Carolina. He and his wife and Frank Hill, and maybe one or two of his clerks, would load up the pop-up camper for the traditional August vacations of most judges and go out West to camp and canoe-raft—to sleep and eat under the stars. But his rafting nearer to home would not take place on the Ocoee River, the site of the white-water rafting competition of the Atlanta Olympics, but rather, as Frank Hill would describe, on the "easier flow" of the Nantahala and Conasauga Rivers of North Carolina.

Sometimes, his August travels would divert to a prison that housed one or more of the prisoners he had sentenced to jail and with whom he had corresponded. His son, Randy, recalls that if one of the vacation travels came near a prison housing any of those prisoners he had sentenced and with whom he had corresponded while they were incarcerated, he would stop and share some time with them.

Another facet of the personality of Frank Wilson was his frugality. He did not believe in borrowing. He bought his home for cash, and when he became a judge, he spent the government's money as if it were his own. As an example, he installed only one telephone line in his chambers even though he could have had multiple lines, and he shared that one with Mrs. Gannaway, his executive assistant. Mrs. Gannaway often had church calls to make on a Monday morning to parishioners who had missed the Sunday worship service. Judge Wilson would wait patiently until he saw the light go out on the phone, which indicated that Mrs. Gannaway was through with her church calls, before making his calls.

His concern for cost was also reflected in his keen awareness of the expense of litigation and how the cost of trials and trial preparation had begun to spiral. He often challenged lawyers to become more cost-effective by working together to identify the real issues that were for trial and thereby shortening not only the preparation process but also the trial itself.

His meals were simple, often taking lunch with his good friend Bill Spears at a downtown Chattanooga cafeteria known as the Home Plate, which no longer exists. And although his dress was not flashy, he did have a summer robe that Helen made for him—a special robe that only went to his waist.

Other than his deep interest in history, he enjoyed classical music and his not-so-classical trombone, which he had played since his high school band and with which he would often retire to the basement to play. He appreciated classical music, not only lying in the living room but also lying on a blanket listening to the Pops in the Park by the Chattanooga Symphony Orchestra or going to Memorial Auditorium for a travelogue.

But all his relaxation did not prevent him from religiously performing his chores. He not only did all the outside chores at his own house—mowing the grass and raking the leaves—but he also regularly mowed the grass at his church, Signal Mountain Methodist Church.

His humor, however, was singular. It was dry, and anyone or anything was fair game, even the Court of Appeals. When he was still in private practice, he gave an assignment to a young lawyer to find a case he could use in a brief on a point of law. After a week, when the young lawyer said he couldn't find such a case, he took over the brief himself. When he, himself, couldn't find a case on the point he needed, he simply wrote in the brief, without the benefit of the case, "The law is so well settled as to need no citation that…"

His collection of anecdotes started early on, and he kept them in a handwritten joke book he used in 1952 in connection with his political forays. Two are worth relating.

It seems that a young boy was sent to fetch some fresh water from a lake. When he returned with the empty pails, he told the man who had sent him that he couldn't get the water because the lake was full of alligators, and he was afraid of the alligators. That man told him that those alligators were more afraid of him than he was of them. The boy replied, "If that's so, that water ain't fit to drink."

In another, an Episcopalian priest, in his clerical garb, was speeding down the highway with his wife and pulled over by a highway patrolman. When the patrolman saw his collar, he admonished the priest, "Father, just slow down. You'll make it to your service on time." As he drove off, his wife turned to him and said, "He thought you were a Catholic priest," to which he said, "Yes, and I wonder who he thought you were."

The humor he had was also seen in the cases that he tried. In one case, when a lawyer lost one of the first jury trials in the asbestosis litigation, where the injury allegedly suffered by the plaintiff was asbestosis, the plaintiff's lawyer was moping back in chambers after the jury returned its verdict in favor of the defendant. Judge Wilson consoled the lawyer by saying, "Jerry, don't be so glum. The jury just told your client he didn't have asbestosis."

In the middle of another case, during the cross-examination of one of the executives of the corporate defendant, a particularly damaging document was offered into evidence to which the defense counsel objected. Judge Wilson inquired as to the basis of the objection, to which counsel responded that the document was "prejudicial." Judge Wilson responded, "Of course it is. Why do you think he's trying to get it in? Overruled."

In a medical malpractice case, an expert witness for the plaintiff was asked to concede on cross-examination by defense counsel that a medical procedure, in any case, was a matter of judgment by the doctor, which should not be questioned because there were always two different ways to diagnose or treat. When counsel for the plaintiff attempted to use the illustration of two cars starting from the same point in reaching their destination by different means, he was interrupted by an objection that the question was argumentative. Judge Wilson started to agree, stating that if the question was going to be if one of the cars didn't arrive, it would be reasonable to conclude something went wrong. It would be objectionable because the answer was obvious. But counsel for the plaintiff said that was not going to be his question. He said his question was going to be, "If two cars start for the same destination and one runs off the road, they both wouldn't get there, would they, Doctor?"

In a criminal case, he permitted counsel for a defendant to ask the jury on voir dire if "there was any reason why you could not return a fair and impartial verdict against the government in this case?"

Then there was a criminal case in which the defendant denied any prior convictions. On cross, he admitted to three specific prior convictions. When asked on redirect why he had denied them, he said, "Well, those are things you just don't like to talk about, particularly in a situation like this."

Another case involved an attractive group life insurance, the policy of which had been offered to a company but on condition that all employees had to sign up. There was a lone standout who refused to subscribe, and there was testimony that the other employees told him that if he wouldn't sign up, they would work him over after work. He signed up, and when asked why he didn't do so at first, he said, "This was the first time I had it explained to me."

Sometimes, as everyone knows, it is better not to ask that extra question on cross-examination. Take, for example, the plaintiff who testified on direct that he was terribly injured as a result of the wreck. When asked on cross why he had not told the state trooper who investigated the accident that he had been injured, the farmer responded that he had his mule and his dog with him that day. When the accident happened, the mule and the dog were thrown in two different directions. He said that the trooper first went over to look at the mule, and when he saw what shape he was in, he pulled his pistol and shot him. He said the trooper went to the dog, and when he found what shape he was in, he shot him. He then testified, "He then came over to me and asked if I was hurt."

Finally, we don't know whether the following defendant was in front of Judge Wilson, but he adopted the following exchange in one of his cases. When a defendant appeared before a court and announced his name was General Robert E. Lee Jones, the judge asked what the general stood for. The man replied, "It's like the *Honorable* before your name, Judge. It don't mean a damn thing."

And so we end the description of the life of a man who meant so much to his family, to his friends, to his community, and to the law.

EPILOGUE

We have become familiar with a truly remarkable man who succeeded and might well have authored Rudyard Kipling's admonition to the boy in the poem "If."

> If you can talk with crowds and keep your virtue,
> Or walk with Kings—nor lose the common touch,
> If neither foes nor loving friends can hurt you,
> If all men count with you, but none too much;
> If you can fill in the unforgiving minute
> With 60 seconds of pie's worth of distance run,
> Yours is the Earth and everything that's in it,
> And—which is more—you'll be a Man, my son!

Indeed, Judge Wilson was a special person.

APPENDIX

A SHORT HISTORY OF THE SUPREME COURT

One Hundred eighty years of experience under the United States Constitution have served to create considerable uniformity in the views held by the American people toward the nature and form of their government. Few, if any, of the issues debated at the time of the adoption of the Constitution remain in discussion today. A major modern difference of opinion, however, regarding the nature and form of the American government appears to center around the United States Supreme Court and the proper role that body is to play in the interpretation of the Constitution. On one extreme some appear to hold the view that the American Constitution is a definitive and unchanging basic doctrine of government requiring of the Court only the ability to read the English language. On the other extreme there are those who appear to view the Constitution as so indefinite and uncertain as to mean only what the members of the Supreme Court at any given time may say that it means. As is often the case, the truth may lie somewhere between the extremes. In any event, a short review of the history of the Supreme Court may serve to point the way to a greater consensus on this modern controversy. By way of introduction a few observations regarding the adoption of the Constitution and certain of its provisions are in order.

I

The framers of our Federal Constitution have been praised for producing a document that has proven to be the most enduring fundamental charter of government ever devised by man. Not the least of their accomplishments was that they were able to produce a document that found support among men of such diverse views as Thomas Jefferson on the one hand and John Adams on the other, and to earn the approval of such diverse states as the small New England state of New Hampshire on the one hand and the much larger southern state of Georgia upon the other. A fact not often recognized is that this was achieved in part by judicious compromise and in part by judicious silence in dealing with some of the thornier problems confronting the framers of the Constitution. With regard to those matters on which there was no serious colonial disagreement, the Constitution was a model of clarity. With respect to more difficult matters, such as the question of equal representation of the states in the new government versus representation upon a population basis, compromise was effected. Finally, and with respect to even weightier problems that might well have prevented ratification had specifics been stated, the framers of the Constitution either remained silent or used broad and indefinite language, thereby leaving such problems largely for posterity to settle.

At the time of the ratification no one could be quite sure what was meant by the "contract" clause, nor the "due process" clause, nor what powers were granted unto Congress by the power to make all laws "necessary and proper" for carrying out the other powers of the national government. Certainly no one could see the full meaning of granting Congress the power to "regulate commerce." Even today the last word has not yet been spoken upon the meaning of any of these clauses, particularly the due process clause and the commerce clause. Certainly at the time of ratification no one knew just how the Constitution, together with the laws and treaties made thereunder, were to be the "supreme law of the land" as provided in the Constitution. Had any more definitive effort been made to spell out the meaning of these and other more general clauses of the Constitution, it would seem unlikely that the Constitution would have received approval at the hands of a sufficient number of the states to assure its adoption.

When one considers the clauses in the Constitution whose meaning is uncertain and compares them with those about which there is no need for interpretation, the uncertain clauses exceed the more certain clauses, at least in significance.

In this regard one of the major uncertainties at the time of the adoption of the Constitution was whether it created a league of sovereign states on the one hand or whether it created a nation and an insoluble union on the other hand.

II

Turning to the Supreme Court, its position in the new government was, of all of the branches of the government, the most uncertain. The Constitution had little to say either about the Supreme Court or about the federal judiciary in general. Rather, it merely stated that "the judicial power of the United States," whatever it may be, is to be vested in the Supreme Court and in such inferior courts as the Congress may from time to time establish. The composition of the Court, the number of its members, and much of its appellate jurisdiction was left entirely for congressional decision. While federal judges, including Supreme Court justices, can be removed only by way of impeachment, the grounds for impeachment are left to Congress. Congress can at any time it elects create new justices or judges. While Article III, Section 2, extends the judicial power to a variety of cases, the second paragraph of that section gives Congress power to control the Supreme Court's jurisdiction of appeals from lower courts, thereby significantly qualifying the appellate powers previously granted. Congress thus has within its power, through its right to control the appellate jurisdiction of the Supreme Court, the authority to control the role that the Court is to play in the government of our nation. Moreover, not the least of the powers of Congress in this respect is its absolute control over judicial appropriations.

Thus it was that our nation began its history with a Constitution that left unanswered almost as many questions as it answered, and a Supreme Court whose size, role and function in the new government was altogether uncertain.

III

The Supreme Court as we know it today has gone through three broad historical periods of constitutional interpretation. Conceding that there are variations within the framework, we can nevertheless identify three great periods in American constitutional development: 1789 to the close of the Civil War; 1865 to the "court revolution" in 1937; and 1937 to the present.

From 1789 to the Civil War the attention of the Supreme Court was directed most frequently to the greatest of all the questions left unsolved by the founders -- the nation-state relationship; and the major judicial concern underlying the more important decisions of this era was the preserving of the American union.

The second great period of constitutional history, running roughly from the end of the Civil War to 1937, was a period in which the major interest of the Supreme Court was with respect to the relationship between government and business; with the Court often seeking to afford protection to the business community against governmental encroachment. It was during this period that first the commerce clause and then the due process clause became the bulwark against government intervention in business.

The last period is upon us and was ushered in with the depression, the New Deal, World War II, and political conditions that these represent. With the development of the due process clause to protect property rights and economic liberty, it was not surprising that due process should be conceived of as extending to the protection of other rights and liberties. In any event we now find ourselves in the third era, the era of the Bill of Rights, the rights of the individual, the right to fair trial, the liberty of free expression even of unpopular opinions, the right to vote, the right to public education -- in short, the Civil Rights Era.

IV

Looking more closely to the first era, extending from the founding of the nation to the Civil War, the following are some of the more significant events and decisions.

In 1789, although the Constitution had created a "Supreme Court," no one knew how it would be composed or what its duties would be. Part of these questions were answered by the Judiciary Act of 1789, which provided for six Supreme Court justices and provided for certain appellate jurisdiction. But, of the many questions unanswered, the most important at that time was where the United States would look for the interpretation of the Constitution.

The most important date in the history of the Constitution, the Supreme Court, and possibly of the United States, may well have been the date of the appointment of John Marshall to the position of Chief Justice of the Supreme Court. John Marshall was a strong nationalist and a Federalist and a conservative. His appointment was one of the last acts of President Adams, just before the inauguration of his major opponent, the Democratic, States Rights, Anti-Federalist Thomas Jefferson. Jefferson supporters were in control of Congress. The stature of the Supreme Court was low. To illustrate the feeling, one has only to look at the statement of Chief Justice John Jay when he refused reappointment by President Adams and stated that he had no faith "that the Court could acquire enough 'energy, weight and dignity' to play a salient role in the nation's affairs."

To understand the position in which John Marshall and the Court found themselves with the election of Thomas Jefferson, it is necessary to look back to some of the history of that era. The Federalists, smarting under criticism, had enacted the infamous Alien and Sedition Acts and these in turn called forth the Kentucky and Virginia Resolutions which challenged, in language composed by Jefferson and Madison respectively, the whole doctrine of national supremacy and the unity upon which the very existence of the Supreme Court hinged. The party of Jefferson won the election of 1800 and the victors came to office with a bitter distrust of the national judiciary which had joined in the persecution of the Republicans under the Alien and Sedition Acts. The outgoing Federalists did their part to make a bad situation worse by passing the Judiciary Act of 1801, creating a number of new federal judgships which were hastily filled by Adams and reducing the number of Supreme Court justices from six to five. The Federalists, having lost two branches of the government, hoped to maintain their control nevertheless by entrenching a Pro-Federalist judiciary.

The test of the Court and John Marshall was not long in presenting itself. In 1803 the landmark case of <u>Marbury v. Madison</u>[1] was decided. Madison was the Secretary of State under President Jefferson and had refused to deliver the commission of office to one Marbury who was a last-minute Federalist appointee of President Adams. Marbury sought a mandamus from the Supreme Court ordering that his commission be delivered. It was obvious that an order of such kind from the Court would be ignored by Madison. On the other hand, a failure to order delivery would show weakness and further impair the dignity of the Court. Here was a situation calling for the legal genius that only a John Marshall could furnish. Marshall was equal to the occasion. Marbury's commission, he said, was being illegally withheld from him by the Jefferson administration and a judicial order can appropriately be directed to a cabinet officer when he fails in his duty. However, the Supreme Court is not the proper tribunal to supply Marbury with his remedy to his case, for the Court does not possess original jurisdiction to issue writs of this kind. Although the Judiciary Act of 1789 purported to give the Court such power, that provision was invalid as the Court's original jurisdiction is defined in the Constitution and a congressional act like this one cannot add to the original jurisdiction and is therefore unconstitutional. Mr. Marbury must look elsewhere for relief. Jefferson appeared to win and the Court was in the remarkable position of refusing authority which they could not constitutionally accept. The Court had rejected the power while assuming the right to decide the constitutionality of the act of Congress. This was a good example of

---

1   5 U.S. (1 Cranch) 137 (1803).

Marshall's ability to advance in one direction while his opponents were looking in another.

There followed a period of judicial restraining while the Marshall court survived impeachment proceedings against a Federalist appointed Supreme Court justice, Samuel Chase, in preparation for a similar impeachment attempt against Marshall himself. At the impeachment proceedings, led by the Jefferson administration, the doctrine was advanced that "impeachment is nothing but an inquiry by Congress whether the office of any public man might not better be filled by another." This was rejected by Congress in a close vote.

In 1810, with the impeachment storms over, the Supreme Court struck out again. In the case of Fletcher v. Peck[2], involving the Yazoo land-grant scandal, the Georgia Legislature endeavored to rescind the sale of lands by a former Georgia Legislature. Members of the former Legislature had been bribed into selling what now constitutes Alabama and Mississippi to land speculators at a ridiculously low price. In the meantime, the purchasers had sold to innocent third parties. Although the specific constitutional objection to the Georgia statute is not clear, the case upheld the power of the Supreme Court to review state statutes. In 1816 and again in 1821 the Supreme Court further established itself as a final word on the meaning of the Constitution and the nation was gradually coming to accept the Court's view of its own function.

The single most important case ever decided was McCulloch v. Maryland[3] decided in 1821 with an opinion by Justice Marshall. There the state had levied a tax on note issues of the Bank of the United States, incorporated by an act of Congress. The state argued that the act creating the bank was unconstitutional, that a state could tax within its borders without restraint and that the Supreme Court could not decide the constitutionality of a state statute. The bank was viewed with special dislike by the States Rights advocates. Any decision upholding its claim to exist and denying the states' claim to tax could be counted on to infuriate them. Marshall, utilizing the doctrine already pronounced,

2   10 U.S. (6 Cranch) 87 (1810).

3   17 U.S. (4 Wheat.) 316 (1810).

stated that the Constitution was the product of popular sovereignty and not the states, that the people made the national government supreme by the Constitution, and that Congress had the power to pass laws "necessary and proper" for carrying into effect other powers. He concluded that to allow the state action would destroy a power given Congress. That this was a nation, and not a confederation of states, was established by Marshall as the master doctrine of the American constitutional law. The right of the Supreme Court to disapprove state laws was again reaffirmed and was to become the instrument that was to preserve the Union more surely than anything short of the Civil War itself.

John Marshall had many other significant decisions affecting various constitutional problems. For example, in the case of Gibbons v. Ogden[4], in interpreting the commerce clause, he struck down the state law granting a shipping monopoly to Fulton on the Hudson River, thus laying the foundation for the greatest common market in the world. No other court nor no other man has had so much to do with shaping the destiny of a nation.

From time to time Justice Marshall was compellingly reminded of the fact, as all Supreme Court justices are, that the Court's decrees are backed only by its own prestige and ultimately by the willingness of the President to help enforce them. Toward the end of the first era, the Court overstepped the boundaries of judicial power and endangered the position that it had earned by its decision in the Dred Scott[5] case. Dred Scott, a slave, had been taken by his owner from Missouri into free territory. Upon return to Missouri he instituted a suit contending that by being taken into free territory he became a free man. Instead of resting the opinion upon the ground that Dred Scott could not bring suit since he was not a citizen but property, or upon the ground that the Court was bound by Missouri law, the majority of the Court decided to solve the slavery issue once and for all. The Court held that Congress could not regulate slavery in the states and territories. At this stage in

---

4   22 U.S. (9 Wheat.) 1 (1824).

5   Dred Scott v. Sanford, 60 U.S. (19 How.) 393 (1857).

history the Supreme Court was virtually friendless, as the South was traditionally States Rights and anti-Court and the Court had succeeded in alienating most of the North. The <u>Dred Scott</u> case elected an obscure ex-Congressman President of the United States. Lincoln debated the <u>Dred Scott</u> decision, gained national attention, won the election, and defeated the Court. Thus, judicial indiscretion in 1857 almost destroyed all that Marshall and Taney had built so carefully since 1801, for the issue of slavery was too big and too explosive and men were too human, too emotional, and too violent to permit a peaceful or judicial solution of the problem.

<u>V</u>

The Civil War ended an era of judicial history. While cases still arose involving the relationship between the Nation and the states, as declared by Chief Justice Chase in 1868, the war had settled the proposition that this was "an indestructible Union composed of indestructible States." With the rapid growth of industry in America following the war, the major issues to come before the Court for the next 70 years centered around governmental regulation of business and the permissible extent of such regulation. For 70 years the Court was generally to throw its weight against the movement to regulate business.

Before turning to the more significant cases to come before the Court during the latter portion of the Nineteenth Century, it is appropriate to recall that the Thirteenth, Fourteenth, and Fifteenth Amendments to the Constitution were adopted in the Reconstruction Period following the Civil War. Of particular significance to a history of judicial review in the Supreme Court are the privileges and immunities, due process, and equal protection clauses set forth as follows in the Fourteenth Amendment:

"No State shall make or enforce any law which shall abridge the privileges and immunities of citizens of the United States; nor shall any State deprive any person of life, liberty or property, without due process of law; nor deny any person within its jurisdiction of equal protection of the law."

Whereas the first eight amendments, including the due process clause of the Fifth Amendment, had previously been held to be a restraint only upon the Federal Government, the provisions of the Fourteenth Amendment were expressly made to apply to the states. The broad and general language of this amendment opened up a new era in the history of judicial review.

The <u>Slaughter House Cases</u>[6] of 1873 are one of the landmarks in any Supreme Court history. The background to these cases was that in 1869 a "carpetbag" legislature in Louisiana had passed a law granting a monopoly to a single New Orleans corporation for the slaughter of livestock. Upon thus being put out of business, other New Orleans butchers promptly went to the federal court to set aside the state law. They contended that under the newly adopted Fourteenth Amendment any attempt by a state legislature to grant a monopoly was a violation of their privileges and immunities as American citizens, a violation of their right to equal protection of the law, and a violation of due process. A majority of the Court was not quite convinced that such an interpretation should be placed upon the Fourteenth Amendment and by a vote of five to four rejected the butchers' claims. The majority held that the privileges and immunities clause referred only to certain special rights of national citizenship, such as the right to travel freely and the right to use navigable waters, and not to all of the rights contained in the Bill of Rights. The equal protection clause was held to protect only Negroes in their newly won freedom. Likewise, the state granted monopoly was held not to violate the due process clause, that clause being interpreted as limiting only matters of procedure and not assuring the substantive right of occupational freedom. By these interpretations the Court avoided for the time the job of providing federal judicial protection against state abridgement of all civil rights. Rather, these matters were left to develop more gradually. The regulation of economic affairs, then only in its infancy, was left for a time by the Court to the "political branches of government."

---

6   83 U.S. 36 (1873).

As business grew the movement to regulate business also grew. There were precedents, of course, going back to <u>Gibbon v. Ogden</u>[7], for finding state economic regulations invalid where they encroached upon interstate commerce. The Court proceeded to do this in a series of decisions running down to the turn of the century. For example, in 1886 in the <u>Wabash</u>[8] case the Court effectively foreclosed the states from regulating interstate railroad rates. Even the national government's efforts to regulate rates was stricken down in 1896 in the case of <u>CNO & TP Railroad v. ICC</u>[9]. The Sherman Anti-Trust Act, passed by Congress in 1890 under its constitutional authority to regulate commerce, was held in 1895 not to apply to manufacturing businesses, as the Court concluded that manufacturing did not involve interstate commerce.

As the demand for social justice and business regulation grew, the Congress during the 1890's turned to the taxing power as a means of regulation. In 1894 an income tax law was passed imposing a tax of 2% on incomes in excess of $4,000.00. The Supreme Court struck the law down, holding that it created a "direct" tax that must be apportioned among the states in accordance with population before it could be valid. The ultimate outcome of this struggle, however, was the adoption in 1913 of the Sixteenth Amendment permitting the income tax.

As early as 1877, with the case of <u>Munn v. Illinois</u>,[10] the Court began to depart from their decision in the <u>Slaughter House Cases</u> and to turn to the due process clause as a basis for striking down business regulation. Although the Court declined in the <u>Munn</u> case to hold legislation regulating grain storage rates invalid, it did suggest that "under some circumstances" a statute might be so unreasonable as to be unconstitutional under the due process clause. By 1895 a majority of the Court had come to the view that the concept of due process was not merely a limitation against procedural irregularities, but also prohibited arbitrary and unreasonable economic legislation. The Court

---

7   22 U.S. 1 (1824).

8   <u>Wabash Railway v. Illinois</u>, 118 U.S. 557 (1886).

9   162 U.S. 184 (1896).

10 94 U.S. 113 (1877).

so held in the case of <u>Smythe v. Ames</u>[11] where rates were held invalid as being unreasonable in the Court's view. With the concept of due process having so evolved by the end of the Nineteenth Century, the Court was equipped to play a major part in shaping government policy in the field of business regulation.

VI

During the first 35 years of the Twentieth Century the Court both sustained and struck down legislation based upon the power of Congress to regulate interstate commerce. Little pattern can be found in the decisions in this area. For example, in the case of <u>Hammer v. Dagenhart</u>[12] the Court struck down legislation prohibiting the interstate movement of goods manufactured by child labor, but on the other hand sustained the Pure Food and Drug Act banning interstate shipment of adulterated food. In these and other decisions in this area the Court appears largely to have relied upon its own judgment of what was proper legislation and what was improper legislation.

In <u>Lockner v. New York</u>[13] (1905), the Court struck down a law limiting the hours of work in the baking industry to ten hours per day or 60 hours per week, the Court concluding that this amounted to an unreasonable interference with employment contracts and was therefore a violation of due process. Although many regulatory and welfare measures were upheld and many economic statutes survived judicial review between 1900 and 1930, the number of negative decisions under the Fourteenth Amendment grew until it almost doubled during the decade from 1920 to 1930. By the time of the depression and the election of Franklin D. Roosevelt as President in 1933 the Court had built up a formidable set of precedents that it could and did use for judicial supervision of the government-business relationship.

---

11   169 U.S. 466 (1898).

12   247 U.S. 251 (1918).

13   198 U.S. 45 (1905).

With the coming of Roosevelt and the New Deal, many new laws designed to regulate and stimulate the national economy were adopted. In a series of decisions in 1935 and 1936 the Supreme Court struck down one New Deal act after another, declaring unconstitutional such acts as the National Industrial Recovery Act, the Bituminous Coal Act, and the Agricultural Adjustment Act. Although the Court passed favorably upon some New Deal legislation, such as the T.V.A. and the Wagner Labor Act, it tore such holes in the New Deal program of recovery legislation that the temper of public opinion in the time was in some ways like that at the time of the Dred Scott decision. It again appeared that the Court had ignored the times and the popular will and as a result had overstepped the bounds of judicial review. In 1937 President Roosevelt proposed legislation that would increase the size of the Court and permit him to appoint six additional justices. This became known as the famous "court-packing plan."

As the battle was being fought in Congress over the court-packing plan, a majority of the Court shifted and in rapid succession approved a Minimum Wage Law, the National Labor Relations Act, and a Social Security Act. This judicial retreat succeeded in defeating the court-packing plan. Shortly retirements from the Court enabled Roosevelt to replace six justices. While Roosevelt lost the battle on his court-packing plan, the depression and the New Deal won the war, largely wiped out 70 years of judicial precedents, and established the right of the Government to direct and control the Nation's economy with a minimum of judicial restraint.

VII

Two eras of Supreme Court history have so far been accounted for. In the first era the Court was primarily concerned with relationships between the Nation and the States. In the second era just recounted, the Court was primarily concerned with relationships between the government and business. In recent years the Court has been primarily concerned with relationships between the government and the individual. The most recent era is therefore often referred to as the "civil rights era."

As previously noted, over the period from 1870 to 1937 the Supreme Court gradually developed an interpretation of the due process clause that made it a principal constitutional protection to property rights and economic liberty. It is not unusual then that the Court should be increasingly confronted with the argument that the due process clause extended to the protection of other rights and liberties. So it has been in recent years, with the result that the present era has become the era of the Bill of Rights, the era of the rights of the individual to a fair trial, to freedom of speech, to vote, and to be free from racial discrimination -- in short the civil rights era.

Even prior to World War II there had been some growing consciousness in America of the injustice of racial discrimination. The racist doctrine of Adolph Hitler prior to and during World War II contributed to a developing awareness among the American people of their own problems of racial discrimination. But long ago, in 1896, in the case of Plessy v. Ferguson[14] the Court created its own major obstacle to the elimination of racial discrimination. There the Court had announced that the races could be legally separated so long as facilities were equal. For the next 50 years the emphasis was upon the existence of separate facilities, with little attention paid to how "equal" they were. The first significant departure from the Plessy rule came in 1938 in the case of Missouri v. Canada.[15] There Missouri had never provided a Negro law school, but rather followed the practice of paying the tuition for resident Negro law students to attend law schools in other states. The State contended that it did not have sufficient Negro law students to justify setting up a separate Negro law school. The Court, stating that the duty to provide equality doesn't depend upon the number of persons who are discriminated against, held that "equal" meant "equal." Missouri was required to admit Negro students into its law schools.

---

14   163 U.S. 537 (1896).

15   305 U.S. 337 (1938).

Over the next 16 years, while not striking down the separation of races permitted under Plessy, the Court continued to place emphasis upon the necessity of the states providing equal facilities. Finally, in 1954 in Brown v. Board of Education,[16] the Court concluded that separate facilities were inherently unequal and thus violated the equal protection clause of the Constitution. Plessy v. Ferguson was overruled and racial separation in the public schools was to be abolished with "all deliberate speed." In 1969 "all deliberate speed" became "now" in the case of Alexander v. Holmes.[17]

In the area of voting rights, the most significant decision of recent years is the case of Baker v. Carr,[18] decided in 1962. Previous to that time the Court had consistently held that the malapportionment of elective bodies was a political matter and therefore not subject to adjudication in the federal courts. In Baker v. Carr the Court reversed its position and held that federal courts have jurisdiction over cases involving the elective process and that state or local elective bodies that are not apportioned according to population violate the equal protection clause. By subsequent decisions the Court has adopted the rule of "one man one vote" as the test to be applied in determining whether an elective body is constitutionally apportioned. The rule has been applied to all types of state and local elective offices.

In a series of decisions in the last decade the Court has accomplished a number of far reaching changes in the field of criminal law. Historically the various limitations contained in the Bill of Rights have been held to apply only to the federal government and not to the states. This proposition was expressly stated as early as 1833 in the case of Barron v. Baltimore.[19] In recent years the argument has been advanced with increasing frequency that the due process clause of the Fourteenth Amendment had the effect of incorporating the various rights set forth in Amendments One through Eight. As early as 1925, when

16   347 U.S. 483 (1954).

17   396 U.S. 19 (1969).

18

19

confronted with a New York law punishing criminal anarchy, the Court had declared, "We may and do assume that freedom of speech and of the press are protected by the due process clause of the Fourteenth Amendment from impairment by the States." Although a majority of the Court thereafter continued to refuse to accept the adoption theory, Justice Black began advancing it in a series of dissenting opinions in the field of criminal law. Finally, starting in 1961, the first of a series of decisions was handed down in which a majority of the Court began the process of extending the Bill of Rights to the states through the due process clause of the Fourteenth Amendment. The case of Mapp v. Ohio[20] in that year concluded that the concept of due process included the Fourth Amendment bar against unreasonable searches and seizures, and that evidence obtained by means of an illegal search was inadmissible in the state courts the same as in the federal courts. Since Mapp v. Ohio the Court in a rapid sequence of cases has found that the due process clause of the Fourteenth Amendment incorporated the concept of one amendment after another of the Bill of Rights, thereby making substantially uniform throughout the 50 states of the Nation the basic ground rules for conducting criminal trials. In 1962, in the case of Gideon v. Wainwright,[21] the Court found that the Sixth Amendment right to counsel in criminal trials extended to the states through the Fourteenth Amendment. This right to counsel was further enlarged in 1964 and 1966 in the cases of Escobedo v. Illinois[22] and Miranda v. Arizona[23] so as to ban the admission of a confession obtained where legal counsel had been denied to the accused. In 1967 due process was held to incorporate the Sixth Amendment right to counsel and the Fifth Amendment prohibition against self-incrimination so as to prohibit the denial of these rights in juvenile proceedings in the state courts. By 1970 the dissenting opinions of Justice Black in the 1940's and 1950's had become the accepted view of a majority of the Court

---

20

21

22

23

with almost all of the Bill of Rights now being held applicable to the states through the due process clause of the Fourteenth Amendment.

Whether the era of rapid developments in the field of civil rights has begun to slow and whether the Court is entering upon a new era of constitutional interpretation can only be told after the decade of the 1970's has run its course.

ABOUT THE AUTHOR

The author is a native of Chattanooga, Tennessee, and a retired trial judge with twenty years of experience on the civil bench and over twenty years of experience as a trial attorney. He tried a number of cases in front of Judge Wilson, one of which was the longest civil jury trial in the Sixth Federal Judicial Circuit. His education was at the University of North Carolina and University of Michigan Law School. His professional involvement has included service on the governing body of the Litigation Section of the American Bar Association and in the House of Delegates of the Tennessee Bar Association. He is a fellow of the American, Tennessee, and Chattanooga Bar Foundations, and his community service includes serving as president of the following organizations: Chattanooga Chamber of Commerce, Chattanooga Rotary Club, Brock-Cooper American Inns of Court, and the Tennessee Safety Council.

CPSIA information can be obtained
at www.ICGtesting.com
Printed in the USA
BVHW071912160720
583883BV00001B/129

9 781984 579317